MARSH DWELLERS OF THE
EUPHRATES DELTA

LONDON SCHOOL OF ECONOMICS MONOGRAPHS ON SOCIAL ANTHROPOLOGY

Managing Editor: Charles Stafford

The Monographs on Social Anthropology were established in 1940 and aim to publish results of modern anthropological research of primary interest to specialists.

The continuation of the series was made possible by a grant in aid from the Wenner-Gren Foundation for Anthropological Research, and more recently by a further grant from the Governors of the London School of Economics and Political Science. Income from sales is returned to a revolving fund to assist further publications.

The Monographs are under the direction of an Editorial Board associated with the Department of Anthropology of the London School of Economics and Political Science.

MARSH DWELLERS OF THE EUPHRATES DELTA

S. M. SALIM

LONDON SCHOOL OF ECONOMICS MONOGRAPHS ON SOCIAL ANTHROPOLOGY

Volume 23

Routledge
Taylor & Francis Group

LONDON AND NEW YORK

First published 2004 by Berg Publishers

Published 2020 by Routledge
2 Park Square, Milton Park, Abingdon, Oxon OX14 4RN
605 Third Avenue, New York, NY 10017

First issued in paperback 2021

Routledge is an imprint of the Taylor & Francis Group, an informa business

© S. M. Salim 2004

Notice:
Product or corporate names may be trademarks or registered trademarks, and are used only for identification and explanation without intent to infringe.

Publisher's Note
The publisher has gone to great lengths to ensure the quality of this reprint but points out that some imperfections in the original copies may be apparent.

ISBN 13: 978-0-367-71701-8 (pbk)
ISBN 13: 978-1-8452-0003-9 (hbk)

Foreword

DR Salim's detailed and intimate study of a marsh-dwelling community of bedouin descent on the Lower Euphrates has strong claims on the attention of both social anthropologists and students of social conditions and change in the Middle East.

In the first place it provides one of the very few systematic and carefully documented field studies of the values and social rules whereby the intense solidarity of the patrilineal and largely endogamous kin groups of bedouin society are sustained. Dr Salim shows that these values and obligations have been substantially maintained by the Beni Isad both in their initial adaptation to a new mode of life as sedentary reed-gatherers in a mosquito-infested marsh refuge, and more recently under the stress of new economic temptations from without. Collective insistence at the level of both lineage and clan on compensation for major offences and acceptance by individuals in the offending group that they must all contribute, continually reaffirm the unity of the group in the recurrent settlement of disputes over women and land as well as physical injury and homicide. The continuing economic power of a man over his wives and sons and the authority of a senior over a junior patrikinsman, which are reinforced by endogamous marriage, sustain the sense of joint responsibility within the lineage and inhibit political and economic divergence on the part of individuals.

But this study also shows that as between clans and lineages in Marsh Arab society as a whole, there have been great changes over the past generation. It analyses the processes whereby a once strongly stratified and authoritarian society has, in the course of increasingly effective external control and the introduction of new economic incentives, become a more open field of competition for status and prestige. The shaikh, who once had prescriptive right to dominate politically and economically both his own chiefly clan and through it the rest of the tribe, is gone. The slaves have been freed of economic disabilities and iron-workers may no longer be openly despised. A few of the Beni Isad have succeeded in taking advantage of new opportunities with the growth of external trade to become comparatively wealthy shopkeepers, moneylenders and exporters. But those who have taken up new and more lucrative occupations have great difficulty in securing recognition as notables, the respected status that is ascribed to the conservative heads of united lineages. These notables scorn the pursuit of personal gain and restrict their economic activities to the ill-rewarded mat weaving necessary for a bare livelihood. For nothing in the marshes has been acceptable as replacing the old prestige of camel breeding. Fishing and dairying, both of which, as despised immigrants have shown, could be materially rewarding, are rejected as unworthy.

But although the old bedouin values are still asserted in an attempt to stem the tide of commerce and external influence, the conflict between new and old values and its repercussions on the solidarity of lineages and the community as a whole are increasing. In 1953, when Dr Salim lived and worked there, ech-Chibayish presented very clearly, in its exceptional and harsh environment, a crucial phase in those processes of technical, economic and social change that are inexorably transforming village communities in the Arab world. His pertinacity in carrying through a year-long study under such difficult physical conditions and his success in establishing such close rapport with opposed factions, was doubtless due in considerable measure to a deep interest in the life of the Marsh Dwellers which goes back to his youth, for he was born in Amara, a town on the edge of the Tigris marshes. When he began his anthropological studies in London in 1950 he looked forward to the possibility of undertaking field research among them. Through this book we are enabled to share in his satisfaction at having carried out so successfully what proved to be an arduous and complex task. The skill with which he has analysed the changing structure of this marsh village and traced the sources of old and new attitudes is a testimony of the good use to which he has put his anthropological training. It is also to be hoped that it will encourage further and equally rewarding field research on other village communities in Iraq.

University College London   DARYLL FORDE
February 1958

Acknowledgments

FOR the invaluable help and guidance offered to me during my studies and in the writing of this book, which is based on my doctoral thesis, I should like to express my most sincere thanks and profound gratitude to my teachers, Professor Daryll Forde and Dr Mary Douglas, of University College, London, without whose assistance it could not have been completed.

I am deeply indebted to many friends in ech-Chibayish, officials and villagers, to all of whom I express my warmest thanks. My gratitude is particularly due to the late Abdil-Hadi Ahl Khayūn, the *sirkal* of Ahl ish-Shaikh clan, who, despite ill-health and heavy responsibilities, sponsored my work and by effective support and valuable information did everything within his power to help me.

To Tariq Ahl Khayūn I owe more than to anyone else in ech-Chibayish for his cordial and constant help. He was my chief and most valuable informant and it is to his active co-operation and deep understanding of tribal life that I owe the greater part of the knowledge that I gained in ech-Chibayish.

S. M. S.

London
April 1955

Editorial Note

THE Editorial Board is most grateful to the Ministry of Education of Iraq, and to the Cultural Attaché of the Iraqi Embassy in London, for providing a grant towards the cost of publication.

We are also indebted to the following persons, who have assisted in abridging and preparing Dr Salim's thesis for publication: Dr Mary Douglas, Professor D. Forde, Mr Robin Horton, Miss Kay Attwood, Mr John Hartley, Mr T. F. Mitchell, Mr T. M. Johnstone, and Mrs M. Horn. The transliteration of Arabic words always presents problems. In this case Dr Salim's wish that the dialect pronounciation should be suggested in the English spelling complicated the issue. Foɪ reasons outside our control, we have not been able to consult Dr Salim as much as we have wished. Final decisions have therefore been taken without his permission. All long vowels are indicated by a line above the letter, thus: ā, ī, ū. There is one exception to this. Two Arabic words, which may both refer to groups with a patrilineal base or core and should strictly be distinguished in transliteration as āl and ahl, have both been transliterated ahl. Those wishing for more precise information on questions of the language used in ech-Chibayish are referred to the Arabic version:

Shākir Mustafa Salīm, *Ach-Chibayish: dirāsah anthrūpūlūjiyyah li-qaryah fi ahwār al-'Irāq*, Baghdad, 1956-7.

CONVERSION TABLE FOR IRAQI MEASURES

1 Iraqi dinar	= 1000 fils	= £1
1 habil	= 0·62 acres / 0·25 hectares	
1 mann	= 198 lb. / 90 Kg.	
1 wijia	= 8·2 lb. / 3·75 Kg.	

Contents

Plates

(between pages 70-71)

MAPS AND DIAGRAMS

PART ONE

Introductory

Introduction

WHEN the Iraqi government entrusted me with the first anthropological field investigation to be carried out in Iraq, I chose to make a study of the inhabitants of the Euphrates Delta. This is largely peopled by descendants of bedouin immigrants, who have adapted themselves in one way or another to life in the marshes. I made a general survey of marsh-dwelling communities in both the Euphrates and Tigris marshes, and used this as a background for a detailed investigation of one large community.[1]

Having chosen the village of ech-Chibayish for intensive study, I had to find a dwelling, transport, servants, food and reliable informants, not easy in marshland conditions. For a dwelling, I had to rent an island on which to build my reed hut. For transport I bought a little canoe, but as it was unsafe in high water, I had to rely on larger hired vessels for much of my travelling. As it is against tribal traditions to work for wages, it took me nearly three months to secure a good servant paddler and I never found a cook. For food I relied on the village school caretaker who used to cook for some of the teachers.

My major difficulty was the suspicious attitude of the people. Only after three months did I feel the community begin to open out to me. I began to find willing informants and was admitted to any guest house. After about six months, they talked about me as one of themselves. The friendship of the head of Ahl ish-Shaikh clan and of his son were invaluable.

Wherever possible, I participated fully in village life, visiting guest houses and village administrative officers, and I made daily tours in my canoe. I obtained life-histories, and used questionnaire and discussion techniques, with discreet cross-checking of any information obtained. I made a detailed census of 120 families.

My investigations took me to Basra and Baghdad, and to Sūg ish-Shyūkh and in-Nasriya. At Basra I visited the date-packing stations for a week. In Baghdad I obtained some published materials, together with a few statistics and official data from the government offices. I visited Shaikh Salim Ahl Khayūn, the ex-shaikh of Beni Isad, who lives temporarily in Baghdad. We had long discussions and I took down from him a lengthy autobiography. At Sūg ish-Shyūkh and in-Nasriya I consulted some official documents and had discussions with administrative officers.

I made frequent short trips to the more accessible parts of the Euphrates marshes, such as il-Abid, Obū Saibaya, Lishan, il-Hammar, Beni Msharraf,

[1] In the village of ech-Chibayish, from 2 January to 24 December 1953.

Iabada, and Sūg ish-Shyūkh, and two long tours to Hor il-Hammar and
the Tigris marshes, each of which took about a month. Nearly every community in the three big marshes of the Tigris region was visited. These
tours enabled me to form a general idea of the Marsh Dwellers and their
distribution, and provided a basis for comparison.

My intensive study of ech-Chibayish revealed a community remarkable
as much for its pride as for its poverty. Pride in tribal traditions, inherited
from bedouin forebears, leads them to despise occupations which would
make their life less hard and precarious. They despise all trade and,
though forced to live by the export of reed mats, they would be ashamed to
produce other goods for sale to each other. Although abjectly poor and
perennially in debt, they leave the natural food potential of their marshes
largely unexploited, and buy what they consume at exorbitant prices from
itinerant traders.

This pride and utter contempt of all trade makes their adjustment to
modern market conditions all the more painful. The community is divided
into those who uphold tribal traditions, who maintain guest houses and
dispense free-handed hospitality, and those who have become business
men. The latter live in separate parts of the village, build different houses,
eat different food. The traditionalists drink coffee, the moderns drink tea.
The business men meet to gossip about business, the tribesmen meet to
arrange compensation for offences, and the marriages of their girls. The
business men are preoccupied with gain; the tribesmen with status. The
solidarity of clan and lineage is, however, still immense, and even those
who have forsaken tribal traditions in other respects, pay the same contribution as others to the levies which are made for communal lineage or clan
obligations.

Although this study was made in the peculiar environment of the
marshes, much of what I record is also valid for other rural communities
in South Iraq. Clan and lineage organization, corporate responsibility for
offences, endogamous marriages, contempt of trade, and love of hospitality,
vary little, whether in the marshes, in the desert zones, or in the rich
arable plains.

I

The Iraqi Marsh Dwellers

THE Iraqi Marsh Dwellers occupy the low-lying country in the
south basin of the twin rivers, the Tigris and the Euphrates. Their
home lies roughly within a triangle drawn between Basra in the
south and il-Kut and il-Kifil in the northeast and northwest. This area is
not a continuous marsh; and much of the population inhabits the numerous towns and villages along the banks of the Tigris and Euphrates. There
are also nomadic tribes of bedouin, who pasture their camels and cattle in
the plains between Amara and il-Kut, in the two desert barriers dividing
the marshes, or west of the Euphrates, between in-Nasriya and il-Hilla.

To the north the marsh region is bounded by the towns of il-Kut on the
Tigris and il-Hilla on the Euphrates; to the south by Basra; to the east by
the Iranian border, which runs for some distance through the marshes; and
to the west by the river Euphrates between il-Hilla and Sūg ish-Shyūkh,
and the southern edge of Hor il-Hammar from Sūg ish-Shyūkh to Basra.

The climate of Iraq is characterized by large diurnal and annual ranges
of temperature, low humidity, and low rainfall. In the southern plains
temperatures range from a cool winter to a very hot summer. The coldest
months are December, January and February, when the mean daily temperature varies between 50°F and 56°F. From March onwards the temperature rises steadily until the hottest months of the year, July and August,
when the mean daily temperature is about 95°F. Temperatures may exceed 120°F during the day, yet at night they may fall to 65°F. From
September the temperature drops steadily, and by the end of November
the winter has set in and frosts may occur.

The rainy season lasts from October to May, and during the rest of the
year there is practically no rainfall. The mean annual rainfall is 200 mm.
(8 inches). The prevailing wind is the *shim l*, or north wind, which comes
from the mountains of Asia Minor and Kurdistan, and sweeps almost con-
tinuously down the valleys of the Tigris and Euphrates; in summer it
mitigates the great heat.

The marshland of southern Iraq is probably one of the largest in the
world. With the alternating stretches of bare desert, it has been estimated
to cover as much as 20,000 square miles.[1] The whole country is built up on

[1] L. Dimmock, The Waterways of Iraq. *Journal of Royal Central Asian Society*,
1945.

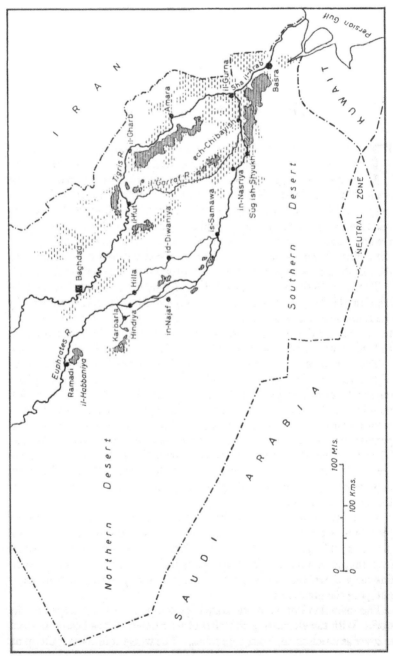

Southern Iraq

the old bed of the sea and is formed by silt brought down by the twin rivers. Much of this potentially fertile plain cannot at present be cultivated, because its soils have a high saline content. The country is completely flat, the only elevations in the whole marsh region being occasional mounds which are thought to be the sites of ancient towns.

From March to July, when the Tigris and Euphrates are in flood, about 4,000 square miles are inundated and become almost one sheet of water, with borders and shallower parts of marsh. When the waters subside, these shallow marshes become dry land, and the former sheet of water becomes a marsh, with large permanent lakes.

Except in the deep water, the marshes are thickly covered with reeds, bulrushes, and floating water-plants. Fish and waterfowl abound. The depth of water over much of the marshes is between four and five feet; in places it is much deeper, and at one spot in Hor li-Hwaiza a depth of nearly twenty feet has been measured. The area of permanent marsh is probably not more than three-quarters of the flood-time marsh.

The three great marshy areas are the Tigris belt, the Hammar belt, and the Euphrates belt. The Tigris belt lies east of the river, and extends almost from Basra to il-Kut; the main marshes are Hor li-Hwaiza, Hor es-Saniya, Hor Ladhaim and Hor Oda. The Hammar belt extends from Gurmat Ali (about five miles north of Basra) to Sūg ish-Shyūkh, Albu Salih and ish-Shatra, around the lower reaches of the Gharraf. In this area the main marsh is Hor il-Hammar. The Euphrates belt extends from il-Khidhir to il-Kifil and is composed of a number of small lakes between the two branches of the Euphrates, the il-Hilla and the il-Hindiya.

Two desert barriers divide the marsh belts; one lies between the Gharraf and the Tigris, and the other between the Gharraf and the Euphrates.

HISTORY OF THE MARSH DWELLERS

All the big tribes of Marsh Dwellers trace their descent from one or other of the well-known tribes of Arabia, who, they claim, migrated to Iraq some time between the Arabian conquest of the country during the reign of Omar, the second Caliph (A.D. 637), and a date which may be as recent as 200 years ago. Their claims are not entirely consistent with the views of archaeologists and anthropologists. When he visited the marsh area and wished to know the relationship of the Marsh Dwellers to the surrounding Arabs, Henry Field recalled 'the theory that the Marsh Arabs are the direct descendants of the Sumerians who lived in Iraq about 5,000 years ago, and that they were driven into the marshes for protection . . .'.[1] Where did Henry Field hear of this theory? He does not state, nor do we know, whom exactly he means by 'Marsh Arabs'.

Henri Frankfort considered the Iraqi marshes to have been already settled in the fifth and fourth millennia B.C. When the northern diluvial

[1] H. Field, Marsh Arabs of Iraq, *Asia*, August 1936.

plains of Iraq which 'had been farmed already for many centuries' were in their third cultural phase 'men from the Persian plateau entered the southern marshes. Under present conditions it would be inconceivable that highlanders would elect to do so, or even that they would be able to survive there. But in the fifth and fourth millennia B.C. the Iranian plateau had not yet become a salt desert. Many rivers, descending from the surrounding mountains, ended in upland seas without an outlet and ringed by swamps. Even to-day, in eastern Iran, marsh dwellers are found on the shores of the great lake of the river Hamun. Like the Marsh Arabs of southern Iraq, they build boats and huts of reeds, fish, and keep water buffaloes and cattle.'[1] Frankfort's opinion was based on archaeological evidence, as 'The pottery made by the earliest settlers of South Mesopotamia shows that they came from Persia.'

Another archaeologist, Seton Lloyd, supports this view. 'It would be a fallacy, however, to imagine that all the cultivators of southern Iraq are provided by the gradual settlement of nomadic Arabs. Any anthropologist who has watched a brachycephalic Mesopotamian *fellah* patiently trenching his field with the identical spade which appears in Assyrian reliefs or carrying home on his shoulder the elementary wooden plough of Sumerian drawings, must realize that this Iraqi at least has his roots in the pre-Arab past of the country.'[2]

In another work Seton Lloyd gives further grounds for his opinion. Speaking about the marsh Arabs he states that 'Their life and circumstances closely resemble those of the earliest, prehistoric settlers in the drying delta, and the ornate cathedral-like guest houses of their sheikhs, built entirely of reeds and mud, approximate most closely to the earliest representations of proto-Sumerian temples in the fourth millennium B.C.'[3]

In any discussion of the origin of the Iraqi Marsh Dwellers three points must be considered. First, it is essential to distinguish both culturally and racially between an 'Eastern Group' of Ma'dan Marsh Dwellers, Albu Mhammad and other Tigris tribes on one side, and a 'Western Group' of Euphrates non-Ma'dan Marsh Dwellers on the other. Secondly, it is probably safe to assume that the Tigris tribes of Marsh Dwellers have, since remote times, been in close contact with their eastern Persian neighbours while the Marsh Dwellers of the Euphrates have been in contact with their western bedouin neighbours. Thirdly, the whole southern alluvial plains of Iraq were the site of ancient Sumerian and Babylonian kingdoms.

Thus it seems reasonable to suggest that the Marsh Dwellers of Iraq are partly descendants of the Sumerians and Babylonians, although their numbers have been augmented by immigrations and intermarriages with the Persians on the east and the bedouins on the west. Such a view is

[1] *The Birth of Civilization in the Near East*, London, 1951, pp. 44–5.
[2] *Iraq*, Oxford Pamphlets on Indian Affairs, No. 13, Bombay, 1943, pp. 17–18.
[3] *Foundations in the Dust*, Oxford, 1947, p. 20.

consistent with archaeological findings, and explains the physical and
cultural differences between the two distinct groups of Marsh Dwellers as
they exist to-day.

CLASSIFICATION OF MARSH DWELLERS

I shall use the term 'Marsh Dwellers' to include all the inhabitants of the
marshes of southern Iraq, regardless of their origin or type of economy.
The other terms, 'Marsh Arabs', and 'Ma'dan', have been used confusedly
in the past. Iraqi townspeople use Ma'dan, indiscriminately either for the
inhabitants of the marshes, or in the sense of boor or rustic, whether the
subject be a townsman, a countryman or a marsh inhabitant. I shall follow
the usage of the Marsh Dwellers themselves and confine my use of the
word to one section of the Marsh Dwellers only, the buffalo-breeders.

Marsh Dwellers cannot be differentiated on a linguistic basis because
there are only small local changes in dialect. To attempt to distinguish
between bedouin and Ma'dan is useless, since many of the immigrant
bedouin tribes have taken to buffalo-breeding, and have long since severed
any connection with bedouin life. The predominant cultural and physical
bedouin traits among the Marsh Dwellers of the Euphrates region which
distinguish them from the eastern Marsh Dwellers of the Tigris, are due
to long contact with the Arabian desert.

It seems more useful to classify the Marsh Dwellers of to-day on an
occupational basis. This gives three broad divisions: the cultivators, the
reed-gatherers, and the buffalo-breeders. Although in any one region there
are some of all three categories to be found, they are distributed roughly as
follows:

CULTIVATORS	LOCATION
Albu Mhammad	The Tigris Marshes from Amara to il-Kassara, and on the river Mijar.
Ahl Izairij	Between the Provinces of Amara and in-Nasriya on the Mijar Issaghir marshes.
Is-Sūdan	Northeast to Amara town on the river Chihala.
Is-Sowaid	Hor li-Athaim.
Beni Lam (part of Is-Sowaid)	North and northwest of Amara town (mainly in Hor Ode and Hor is-Sandya).
Khafaja	The lower reaches of the river Gharraf.
Albu Salih	Between the lower reaches of the river Gharraf and ech-Chibayish north border.
Il-Mijjara	Sūg ish-Shyūkh district, west of the river Euphrates.
Beni Khaigan	Sūg ish-Shyūkh district, east of the river Euphrates.
Ijazayr	ech-Chibayish and il-Midina districts.

CULTIVATORS	LOCATION
Beni Mansur	Il-Gurna district.
Beni Hachcham	Between ish-Shnafiya and Id-Draji, on the Euphrates.
Khizail, Jbur and Ahl Fatlah	Between the two branches of the Euphrates, il-Hilla and il-Hindiya.

The cultivators who depend primarily on agriculture and secondly on cattle, constitute the vast majority of the Marsh Dwellers. Cultivation is carried out twice a year, when the flood waters allow; in summer the crop is mainly rice and great millet, and in winter, wheat and barley. Vegetables are cultivated in some districts to a considerable extent, for trade with the nearest markets in the villages and towns.

Cattle are kept, especially among the farmers of the Tigris marshes, and their produce is sold. Women usually make daily trips to the nearby markets with milk, butter, cheese and cattle-dung, returning with tobacco, sugar, tea, cloth and other essentials.

REED-GATHERERS	LOCATION
Beni Isad	ech-Chibayish village and il-Kharfiya a few miles down the Euphrates.
Albu Mhammad (Butabta, Nuwafil Ahl Irthayil, Albu Ghannam and Ishshada clans)	Hor il-Kassara.

I shall say much more about the reed-gathering economy below.

BUFFALO-BREEDERS	LOCATION
Albu Mhammad (Bait Nasr Allah and Albu Ghannam clans)	Hor li-Hwaiza.
Il-Bunda	Hor li-Athaim.
Iagail	Ij-Jdwal on the lower reaches of the river Gharraf.
Il-Fartūs	Hor il-Abid.

These Ma'dan depend mainly on their herds of water buffalo. A rich family usually owns between seven and ten beasts, a middle-class one between three and five, and the poor families between one and three. Water buffaloes are highly valued for their dairy products and are not killed or sold, particularly when they are fully grown and productive. Occasionally one-year old oxen are killed and eaten, not so much to provide meat as to leave sufficient fodder for the more valuable cows.

Very little of the milk is consumed fresh. It is usually made into butter or clarified butter and sold to mobile canoe-shops which come to the locality, or is taken to towns and villages to be sold at the markets.

Most of the food of the Ma'dan is bought from the markets of the villages and towns on the fringe of the marshes. Cereals are sometimes obtained, either by bartering dairy products or by working on fields in the rural areas near the marshes in the harvest seasons.

The prosperous families of the Ma'dan do nothing apart from tending their buffaloes. Provided that the numbers of young oxen are kept down, there is no problem in finding sufficient fodder, since the animals feed on the young green reed and bulrushes in the marsh. Moreover, at certain seasons of the year the Ma'dan buy grazing rights in the harvested fields of the farming areas and there cut and store the stems of the crops, usually great millet, as supplementary cattle-feed. A Ma'dan family owning ten head of buffalo can obtain money by selling a number of the young animals each year, and also by the sale of dairy products. The poorer families may also have to undertake mat-weaving, hired labour or (in the case of Hor li-Hwaiza Ma'dan) cultivation; but the secondary incomes, derived from mat-weaving or hired labour, make up but a small proportion of the Ma'dan economy. Fishing is carried on for consumption but not for sale.

DEMOGRAPHY

Unfortunately no official data concerning the population and density of the Marsh Dwellers are available. The only census that has ever been carried out in Iraq was that of 1947 which, based on the administrative divisions, i.e. *liwā* (province), *qaḍā* (a division of a province) and *nāḥiya* (a division of a *qaḍā*), contained no records of the tribal population. We are therefore reduced either to broad guesses or to the estimates of administrative officers, which are little better.

On this basis, the Marsh Dwellers have been estimated at 300,000, but I think they may very well amount to 400,000. To give estimates for the three occupational divisions of cultivators, reed-gatherers and buffalo-breeders is even more difficult and uncertain, but one can say that the cultivators comprise the great majority and may total 350,000. The reed-gatherers and the buffalo-breeders may total about 25,000 each.

The density of population in the marshes is unknown, but that of the provinces in which their home lies, namely Basra, Amara, il-Mintifig, id-Diwaniya, il-Hilla and il-Kut is as follows[1]:

Province	Density per sq. km.
Basra	28·6
Amara	16·4
Il-Mintifig	26·1
Id-Diwaniya	25·7
Il-Hilla	49·5
Il-Kut	14·0

There are four forms of settlement. First, the village (*is-salaf*, or in the Euphrates marshes, *in-nazil*) is usually found in the densely populated

[1] *Statistical Abstract, 1950*, Principal Bureau of Statistics, Ministry of Economics, Baghdad, 1952.

areas, and comprises from 100 to 300 huts. A village usually has one or more guest houses (*muḍif*[1]) and a shop, and is divided into sections occupied by different patrilineages. Villages are scattered along the edge of the main waterways and over cultivated lands.

Secondly, a mound, *ishān*, is an island in the permanent marshes usually taken as a residence either by the reed-gatherers or the buffalo-breeders. A mound settlement is usually composed of a number of huts lightly constructed with reeds or bulrushes. The number of huts varies from 30 to 40 on the small mounds, to 500 on the larger ones. There is at least one shop on each mound, but guest houses are rare. Mounds are occupied usually by one or a number of patrilineages, or sometimes by contingents of different clans. In each of the large permanent marshes (Hor il-Hammar, Hor il-Kassara and Hor li-Hwaiza) there is a number of these settlements.

Thirdly, in the flood season the buffalo-breeders make a raft or floating platform (*id-dibūn*) of reeds, bulrushes and earth. It is large enough to hold a hut, or a few buffaloes, and can be poled from place to place and used as a temporary residence. A group of such rafts may form a settlement which sometimes even has its own shop. These floating islands are found only in Hor il-Hammar and Hor li-Hwaiza, and then in limited numbers.

Lastly, reed islands (*chibāyish*)[2] are raised during the high-flood season by layers of bulrushes, reed and earth, and are used as residences. This is the special form of settlement found at ech-Chibayish village and unique in the marsh region of Iraq.

RELIGIOUS BELIEFS AND CULTS

The Iraqi Marsh Dwellers are Shi'ah Muslims, but they are by no means strict in their religious observance. The focus of their religion is Ali,[3] the Imam, and his male descendants. Though they believe, like other Muslims, in Allah and Muhammad, they have abandoned many fundamental tenets of Islam and concentrate on devotion to the Imams. In addition to the prayers and fast in the month of Ramadhan, which are rarely practised, the rituals observed are: mourning the murder of Husain; pilgrimage; and burial in sacred ground. Mourning the murder of Husain, the second son of Ali, and his followers at the Battle of Karbala[4] consists of organized gatherings lasting ten days, during which chapters of the stirring incidents of the murder are read dramatically to the accompaniment of weeping and beating of breasts.

Pilgrimages to the tombs of Ali (at in-Najaf), Husain and Abbas (at Karbala) and il-Kadhum are among the most sacred rituals. The Marsh

[1] The root is from the word *ḍiyāfah*—'hospitality'.

[2] *chibayish* is derived from the Arabic root (*kbs*) which means 'to tread down', 'to stamp underfoot', or 'to press'.

[3] The Prophet's cousin and son-in-law.

[4] A town on the western side of the Euphrates and about 100 km. south of Baghdad, where Husain was murdered over 13 centuries ago while trying to occupy Iraq.

Dwellers save in order to make one of these pilgrimages, and the returned pilgrim is regarded as a pious man.

In the belief that it will ensure the protection of the Imam Ali, Marsh Dwellers from every corner of the marsh region, however inaccessible, wish for burial in the sacred ground of in-Najaf. If this cannot be done immediately after death, the body may be deposited in local ground until the family can transfer it to the holy burial ground. The Marsh Dwellers believe that a Muslim is assured of immortal residence in Paradise if he has demonstrated his devotion to the Imams (Ali or his male descendants), visited one or more of their holy shrines and is buried at in-Najaf; and assistance in taking their dead to in-Najaf is one of the main obligations of the clan.

CONTACT WITH AND MIGRATION TO TOWNS

Frequent contact between the Marsh Dwellers and the neighbouring towns and villages began only after the First World War, with the penetration of the marshes by the Iraqi Administration and the growth of law and order in the region.

The Marsh Dwellers then began to realize that the markets of the neighbouring villages and towns were profitable places in which to sell marsh products. Their women began to make daily visits carrying mats, reed, buffalo and cattle dung for fuel, dairy products (usually curds, butter and clarified butter), fish, birds and other produce. When this trade proved profitable, they began to spend some of the money earned on luxury articles, such as sugar, tea, tobacco and certain kinds of Manchester cloth. Contact increased steadily until eventually shops were started in the marsh region itself by pioneer townsmen and, later, by Marsh Dwellers themselves who first sold sugar, tea and tobacco, and finally even aspirin, pencils and safety razors.[1] Trade at first was by barter, mainly for mats, cereals and fish, then currency was used as well as barter, according to the convenience of the shopkeepers. Canoes fitted up as floating shops began to tour the remote parts of the marshes.

This trade and constant contact between villages and towns encouraged some of the Marsh Dwellers to consider leaving the marsh temporarily or even permanently. The main inducements were, firstly, the readiness of the Iraqi government in the early 1920's to enlist in its newly formed army and police forces an enormous number of young men. This gave a Marsh Dweller the chance of a new life, very different from his existence in the marsh. Secondly, men and women of the marshes found it profitable to work as porters, night watchmen, building workers and servants in the towns.

These temptations were supported by good reasons for leaving the marshes. During the international slump in cereal prices in the 1920's and

---

[1] Shops in the marsh region are controlled by the shaikhs; very high rents are demanded and the Marsh Dwellers are compelled to buy from these shops only.

the early 1930's, the government was compelled to raise the taxes on produce, a measure which caused a good deal of unrest. The shaikhs passed
these demands to the peasants and exploited them more as government
pressure increased. Attracted by the prospects of gain in the towns, and
driven by the cruelty of the shaikhs, as well as by the low prices offered
for their crops, the Marsh Dwellers emigrated in thousands.

The boom in emigration from the marshes was from 1928 to 1931 and
one result was the spread of prostitution among the immigrant marsh
women and of robbery in the towns where they settled. After 1931 the
difficulty of finding employment in the towns checked the tide of emigration. Another migratory movement has recently begun from the Tigris
marshes, because of exploitation by some shaikhs. Thousands of peasants
have moved to nearby towns and villages, and even to Kuwait. Armed
clashes have occurred for the first time in the history of the marsh between
the peasants and government police forces backing the shaikhs.

ADMINISTRATION

Until the World War of 1914-1918, the Iraqi Marsh Dwellers were almost
completely isolated. Even the Young Turks' policy of reform in Iraq did
not touch the marshes. During the Ottoman rule there was no government
representation of any kind except for a few police stations at the bigger
riverain villages on the fringes of the marsh.

When the 1914-1918 war ended and a new national government was
created in Iraq, administrative centres were established in the villages and
police stations were set up throughout the marshes. Then, in the early
1930's, reed-hut schools were set up, usually with only one teacher. Because
of the support of some parents who wished their children to enjoy the
benefits of education, and of one or two of the shaikhs, this proved fairly
successful and the government was encouraged to open more new schools
and enlarge the old ones. In due course dispensaries were opened in the
big villages and mobile dispensaries in motor launches were introduced to
reach the reed villages in the heart of the marshes. Thus government
activity increased and in the 30 years since the establishment of the Iraqi
government, noticeable progress has been made. To-day the whole marsh
region is included in the administrative system, and the bigger villages
have administrative and medical officers, police inspectors, schools, postal
clerks and sometimes veterinary officers and municipal officials. The
Marsh Dwellers have begun to understand and appreciate the work of the
government and its local services.

Naturally there has been strong conflict between the government, with
its policy of helping the Marsh Dwellers, and the shaikhs, who from time
immemorial have controlled the tribesmen. The powerful shaikhs opposed
all the government's efforts to penetrate the marshes; some even opposed
the establishment of police stations and schools. They realized that such
penetration threatened their interests and authority. The government's

plans for the peasants' welfare were seriously impeded when the shaikhs themselves began to gain high political positions, for some of them became deputies and senators and a few were even made ministers. Many essential reforms, especially those of land settlement, have been delayed for a considerable time because they are against the interests of the shaikhs. This conflict between the interests of the hundreds of thousands of Marsh Dwellers and those of a few influential shaikhs is one of the major problems which the Iraqi Government still has to face.

2

Ech-Chibayish and its Environment

APART from its intrinsic interest as a village composed of 1,600 islands, both practical and theoretical reasons led me to select the village of ech-Chibayish for an intensive study. It is in many ways a typical marsh-dwelling community. It depends mainly on reed-gathering for its livelihood, but a certain amount of cultivation is undertaken whenever climatic conditions permit, and trading relations are maintained with nomadic Ma'dan buffalo-breeders. So from this one centre I was able to observe the main occupational groups and their relations with each other.

For political reasons ech-Chibayish seemed particularly interesting since the abolition of the shaikhdom in 1924, and the relatively strong representation of the central government gave an admirable opportunity for the study of the impact of modern administration. At the same time I was assured of more favourable conditions of work than I could have expected under a shaikh.

LOCATION

Ech-Chibayish is about 20 miles up the river Euphrates north of Il-Gurna, where it meets the Tigris, and about 66 miles north of Basra. It is 20 miles south of Sūg ish-Shyūkh, and about 55 miles south of in-Nasriya. It is situated on the left side of what, many hundreds of years ago, used to be the bank of the river Euphrates, and is now part of the great marsh of Hor il-Hammar.

A few miles south of Sūg ish-Shyūkh the Euphrates loses its identity when it mingles with the great Hor at its western end, and stretches in a vast sheet of water from this point almost as far south as Basra. Though the old channel of the Euphrates can still be seen near ech-Chibayish during the low-water season, it is no deeper nor more navigable than other marsh waterways. During the high-water season when Hor il-Hammar joins with the eastern marshes of the Tigris, the whole locality becomes one vast morass.

THE MARSH

The marsh of Hor il-Hammar is some 70 miles long from the western to the eastern end, where a cut allows it to drain into Shatt il-Arab at Gurmat Ali, near Basra. It is divided by a chain of marshy islands and reed clumps through which there are numerous winding navigable channels.

The eastern part of the Hor il-Hammar is the deeper and contains stretches of open water; it is about 30 miles wide from north to south. The western part is some 15 miles wide, and many of the shallower navigable channels are full of water-weeds which render the use of power-driven craft impossible. The whole area of the Hor il-Hammar is more than 1,500 square miles.

In remote times all this area was under water, being in fact part of what we now call the Persian Gulf, and the twin rivers emptied into it through two distinct mouths. Gradually, however, the silt they brought down filled the shallow head of the Gulf, as in fact it still does to-day; what was sea became salty marsh, the salty marsh in turn became more or less solid ground.

There is historical evidence that the Hor il-Hammar came into existence about A.D. 600. Le Strange[1] called this Hor the Great Swamp, and described how it was formed about the end of the fifth century A.D. during the reign of the Sassanian king Kubath I.

In his day the dykes existing along the Tigris channel, as it then ran, having been for many years neglected, the waters suddenly rose, and pouring through a number of breaches, flooded all the low-lying lands to the south and south-west.

During the following reign the dykes were partly repaired and the land brought back into cultivation, but in about A.D. 636

the Euphrates and the Tigris again rose, and in such flood as had never before been seen. Both rivers burst their dykes in innumerable places, and finally laid all the surrounding country under water.[2]

FLOOD AND IRRIGATION

The regular flooding of the Euphrates is caused by the melting of the snow in the mountains along its upper reaches. This takes place about the beginning of March and increases gradually till the end of May. The river continues high and its course is very rapid for thirty or forty days, but afterwards there is a daily decrease, which becomes very small and regular towards the autumn. From the middle of September to the middle of October, the river is at its lowest ebb; and it seems to be almost stationary until the rains commence towards the end of October, when there is a variable increase which continues till the end of December. From this time till the beginning of March the river is subject to slight variations in size and volume.

The flood has a considerable effect on the lower reaches of the Euphrates because the bed of the river, raised by excessive silting, cannot hold the great volume and floods the whole area from the vicinity of in-Nasriya downwards, causing great losses, especially when it prevents summer

[1] G. le Strange, *The Lands of the Eastern Caliphate*, Cambridge, 1905, p. 26.
[2] Ibid., p. 27.

cultivation in large areas. This has happened nearly every year since the deliberate destruction of irrigation works by the Mongols when they invaded Iraq in the thirteenth and fourteenth centuries. That was a severe blow to almost all the irrigation works in the country. I quote Longrigg.

Most ruinous of Hulagu's acts had been the studied destruction of the dykes and headworks whose ancient and perfected system had been the sole source of wealth. Disordered times, and the very fewness of the spiritless survivors, forbade repair; and the silting and scouring of the rivers once let loose, soon made the restoration of control the remote, perhaps hopeless problem to-day still unsolved.[1]

Other causes have contributed to the present state of flood and irrigation, especially in the southern parts of the Euphrates. Firstly, there is no artificial method of effective control on the river from its source to its mouth, except for the Habbaniya controlled escape and the Hindiya Barrage which regulates the water through its two branches, the Hilla and the Hindiya.

Secondly, a great quantity of water flows from the Tigris to the Euphrates between in-Nasriya and il-Gurna, owing to the fact that the bed of the former river is higher than that of the latter between these two places. This is most obvious in the ech-Chibayish district. There is the permanent continuous Hor extending from the Tigris to the ech-Chibayish district, through which water flows unhindered to the Euphrates, while three of the Tigris branches, the li-Btaira, the Mijar es-Saghir and the Mijar il-Kabir, flow southward towards ech-Chibayish and pour their enormous load of water into the marsh north of ech-Chibayish.

Thirdly, for centuries the inhabitants of the alluvial plains of Iraq have been left completely free to dig channels and streams, build dams, dykes or weirs according to their local needs. This has been carried out on a wide scale in all the cultivating areas, especially the rice-cultivating area of id-Diwaniya Province, its worst effect being on the lower reaches of the Euphrates.

WATERWAYS AND COMMUNICATIONS

The only communication between the village and the outside world is by water. There are several types of water craft. The first are four small motor launches of 25 horsepower, operating down the river between ech-Chibayish and il-Gurna, a journey of about 20 miles.

A large number of canoes navigated by paddle or poled by a stout reed are used to make short trips to the Hor for gathering reeds or to neighbouring communities for trade or passenger transport. Large canoes are used for long journeys to the Amara marshes and the Gharraf and Hor il-Hammar communities. These canoes may have small sails but are usually navigated by poles.

Large sailing boats are used mainly for cargo and sometimes for

[1] S. H. Longrigg, *Four Centuries of Modern Iraq*, Oxford, 1925, p. 13.

passengers. Going up the river one or more of these large boats can be towed by a motor launch, a method used at certain seasons of the year. From ech-Chibayish down to il-Gurna, water communication is open all the year round, and for all types of water craft, but up the river to Sūg ish-Shyūkh it is only possible during the flood season from March to July. During these five months motor launches tow large barges or boats, and ship most of the village's output of mats northwards as far as il-Falloja. Local motor launches carry out occasional trips to Sūg ish-Shyūkh. During the remaining seven months communications up the river are not practicable except for canoes which in certain places, such as il-Maslag, either have to be abandoned and the trip completed on land, or have to be drawn by hand for considerable distances over mud.

In the Hor there are certain well-known channels used for communications between various parts of the Hor and other places by canoes.

Within the village of ech-Chibayish the natives use various types of canoes and boats. These craft are called *maṭor*, *chlaika*, *mashḥoof*, *ṭarrāda*, *kiꞌda* and *balam*, according to their size which varies from 11 to 35 feet. All are made of planks of light wood coated with bitumen, and are paddled, poled, or navigated with sails.

I calculated that there is one craft for every 5·2 persons. In a sample of 120 families, I found that 20 families were without any craft of their own, and 21 had only one craft.

NEIGHBOURING COMMUNITIES

Ech-Chibayish is in close contact with a number of other marsh communities situated on the southern and northern edges or in the Hor il-Hammar itself. The main communities on the southern edge are: ish-Shwariya, ish-Shati, ech-Chirbasi, Ijilā, Slaiyl and Ialiwi.

Ish-Shwariya consists of about 150 families, all of the Beni Isad tribe except about ten families of Ahl Sadūn and their followers under a Sadūni shaikh. The main source of livelihood of the inhabitants is extracting salt from about 50 wells. The salt is sold or bartered for cereals in the neighbouring villages or in the Amara and il-Gharraf districts. During the wet season when salt extraction is prevented by the rains, they fish in the Hor. A few families keep buffaloes. Though the land is fertile and Ahl Sadūn has a water pump for irrigation, the Beni Isad of ish-Shwariya do not practise cultivation and the Ahl Sadūn have to bring in peasants from outside.

Ish-Shati is composed of about 50 families of Beni Isad under a Sadūni shaikh. They cultivate patches of land, extract salt from about 35 wells and four families own some 20 head of buffalo.

Ech-Chirbasi is a peninsula which becomes an island during the flood season. There are 94 huts on it, inhabited by 66 families. Of these families, 63 are of Ahl Wnais, two of il-Hadadiyīn and one of Ahl Khayūn, all of which are clans of Beni Isad. There are more than 50 salt wells which are the main source of livelihood. Most of the salt is bartered in the Amara and il-Gharraf districts for rice and great millet. During September, when fish are abundant, most of the men fish and the catch is usually sold to traders who come to ech-Chirbasi, or is taken to other places to be bartered for dates. During the summer cultivation season the inhabitants cultivate great millet in about 200 acres around their peninsula. There are between 40 and 50 men who practise cultivation, supplying their own seeds and giving one-third of the output to the *sirkal* who holds the land.

Ijilā is an island which lies a few miles from the southern edge of the Hor. There are about 40 families on the island; 30 of them are of il-Hadadiyīn and two of the Ahl Wnais clan of Beni Isad, four families are from il-Midina[1] and the rest are Ma'dan. Salt extraction from 39 wells, the output of which is taken to the il-Gharraf district to be exchanged for cereals, and summer cultivation of great millet, are the sole means of livelihood for this community.

Slaiyl is a ridge of land projecting from the south end of the Hor and occupied by about 1,000 members of il-Halaf tribe. The inhabitants here practise summer cultivation, mainly great millet. Many of the population fish in organized teams of ten to fourteen men, the catch being taken to the Basra markets to be sold. They keep cattle and use their products for domestic consumption only. In years of very high waters, such as 1946 and 1953, most of the ridge is flooded, and the majority of the inhabitants leave it for Ijilā until the water recedes.

Ialiwi is the furthest community on the southern edge. It is very small and the majority of the inhabitants depend on summer cultivation. Two crops are cultivated here; great millet for local consumption and water melon which is taken to Basra for sale.

The northern edge of Hor il-Hammar is inhabited by members of a number of distinct tribes, of which the chief are:

the Beni Isad of ech-Chibayish, who number between ten and eleven thousand and depend in their economy on reed-gathering, agriculture, cattle-breeding and other minor sources of income.

the Beni Htait and Al bu Shama who inhabit il-Hammar village. They practise summer cultivation and migrate in large numbers to il-Gharraf for hired labour during the winter crop harvest season. Some of them go to Basra to work in the date camps.

Ahl Harub, Li-fhūd and Id-dbat, who live in many separate communities scattered over the northern edge of the Hor. All these tribes are cultivators and cattle-keepers and own a large number of date palm trees.

Ahl Ismaīl, Iabada and Beni Msharraf: large tribes the members of which are mostly cultivators and cattle-keepers, but of which many poor

---

[1] A marsh village on the right bank of the old channel of the Euphrates, half way between ech-Chibayish and il-Gurna.

families, especially of Iabada and Beni Msharraf, migrate as hired labourers every year to il-Gharraf and Basra.

In addition, there are many Ma'dan communities composed mainly of Iagail, Sidaida, Dinag, Nowashi and Siraihat, moving in the Hor and taking up temporary residence in various parts of it, usually at Id-dibin and other places on its eastern extremity, to live on the produce of their buffalo herds.

SIZE AND GROUPING OF POPULATION IN ECH-CHIBAYISH

The village of ech-Chibayish is mainly occupied by the Beni Isad, a large and ancient tribe which has branches in various parts of Iraq and in south-western Iran. In addition to Beni Isad, ech-Chibayish contains a number of Ma'dan (Nowashi, Siraihat, and others) either living there permanently or seasonally, and three families of Ṣubba (Mandaeans).

According to the general census of 1947, the inhabitants of ech-Chibay-ish village numbered 9,768, distributed among the main clans found in the village as follows[1]:

Clan	Population
1. Ahl ish-Shaikh	4,500
2. Ahl Ghrïj	1,263
3. il-Hadadiyïn	1,200
4. Ahl Khatir	773
5. Beni Aschiri	625
6. Ahl Anaisi	487
7. Ahl Wnais	450
8. Ahl li-Mabir	315
9. Ahl Wais	155
Total	9,768

This census was, however, carried out in October, when all the labourers in the date camps were still away from ech-Chibayish, and so about one thousand persons were not counted. The total population of ech-Chibayish is, therefore, approximately eleven thousand souls.

As far as I could ascertain, there has been no immigration into ech-Chibayish in the last ten years. The majority of 'strangers' living there came before the abolition of the shaikhdom in 1924. On the other hand, many inhabitants have left the village in the last 30 or 40 years. Emigration from ech-Chibayish is not due to land tenure problems or to exploitation by the shaikhs, as was the case among the Marsh Dwellers of Amara; rather, the main reasons seem to have been the ruin of agriculture by high floods and the consequent difficulty of earning a living.

There used to be about 150 families of Ṣubba[2] at ech-Chibayish, living mainly as blacksmiths and canoe-builders. But in the period of political

[1] Census of Iraq, 1947, Directorate General of Census, Baghdad, 1954.
[2] On the Mandaeans, see Chapter 6.

disturbances in the villages between 1915 and 1925 some of Ahl Khayūn, the noble clan of Beni Isad, treated the Ṣubba families very harshly, imposing heavy taxes and even plundering their property. Gradually they began to leave ech-Chibayish, and in 1953 there were no more than three families of Ṣubba in the village.

Another migration seems to have taken place during one of the long wars with the Ottoman government when the great majority of the tribe, driven out of its territory by the Ottoman army, migrated to li-Hwaiza in Persia for several years. As a result of this war, some of Beni Isad remained in Persia and others took up residence at Gurmat Ali, a village a few miles north of Basra.

The majority of Beni Isad who have migrated from ech-Chibayish recently are now living at the other edge of Hor il-Hammar, at ish-Shati, ish-Shwairiya, ich-Chirbasi and Ijilā, and at Margīl, on the outskirts of Basra. But there are no data concerning the date of their migration, or the number of migrants.

The detailed distribution of the clans of Beni Isad in the village can be seen from the map opposite. It will be seen that the greater part of most of the clans form territorial blocs, though minorities of some clans form enclaves in the majority blocs of others.

There are a few families of Ma'dan living to the north of the Ahl Khatin clan, between Gurmat Bhaima, Gurmat Msallam and il-Midar il-Fogani. Two of the three families of Ṣubba live among the il-Hadadiyīn clan, on Gurmat Um ij-Jithūa, and the third family lives with the Ahl Ghrīj clan on Gurmat Liawaija.

LAY-OUT OF THE VILLAGE

The village consists of about 1,600 little islands stretching in a long narrow belt more than three miles in length but only 50 to 150 yards in width. The lay-out is shown diagrammatically on the map opposite.

Ech-Chibayish consists of two distinct but unequal sections: in-Nahiya and in-Nazil. In-Nahiya is a small central section of the village which has been reclaimed by the successive raising of the surface of the islands, and the damming of little streams and creeks which separate some of them, to form a larger stretch of land. This was the site of the residence and guest house of the later shaikhs of the tribe, and afterwards became the site of the in-Nahiya (local district) government offices. It is now 615 yards in length, but no more than 50 yards wide. There is a brick embankment along the river front with two brick bridges built over two small streams, Gurmat ish-Shurta and Lughmaija, the first at the western and the second at the eastern end of this section. The brick-built part is 454 yards in length beginning from the western bridge. It is composed of 24 private houses, a few built and owned by the government, the majority of which are occupied by the village officials and teachers; the government house, the dispensary and the school; and the village market, consisting of 65 shops. The re-

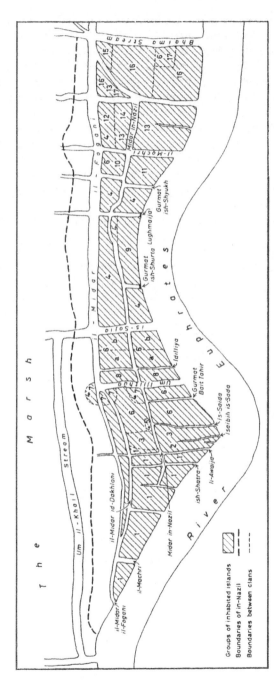

Ech-Chibayish village, distribution of clans

In order to show the distribution of groups of islands occupied by the various clans, the transverse scale on the map has been distorted and distances between the marsh and the river greatly exaggerated. The distance along the river from Gurmat Bhaima to Hamrawia stream is more than three miles, while the distance from the river to the boundaries of in-Nazil is only 100 to 150 yards.

c

maining 161 yards between the end of the brick-built part and the western bridge are occupied by a few reed huts.

In-Nazil[1]—the rest of the village—is composed of small islands separated from the Hor by one long channel running parallel with the river, and from each other by about twenty streams running from north to south, from the marsh to the river. The islands are small and their size varies considerably from high to lowwater seasons. The smallest island is about 60 square yards in area, while the large islands may be as big as 200 square yards. During the lowwater season many groups of the islands form continuous stretches of land and there is water only in the main channels; but during the highwater season nothing is to be seen but huts and guest houses emerging above the water with some palm-trunk bridges joining the various parts of the homesteads.

There are two channels running parallel with the river. The Midar in-Nazil stream flows almost the entire length of the village from east to west, dividing in-Nazil into two nearly equal parts, and intersecting all the channels which flow from north to south. The second channel, il-Midar il-Fogani, forms the northern border of the in-Nazil and runs from the west, from the beginning of in-Nazil, to the east, far beyond the eastern edge of the village.

[1] *In-Nazil* among the Marsh Dwellers of the Euphrates means a stretch of inhabited territory.

PART TWO

Social Organization

3

Political Organization, Past and Present

THE OLD FEUDAL SHAIKHDOM

DURING the four centuries of the Ottoman occupation of Iraq, which came to an end with the First World War, the tribes of the marsh region never knew effective administration; the farther a given area from Baghdad, the more tenuous the control exerted over it by the provincial government.

Only during the last four or five decades of their domination, particularly from the time of Midhat Pasha, the Wali[1] of Baghdad (1869-1872) did the Turks establish a few scattered gendarmeries here and there, and set up administrative centres in towns and the bigger villages in the region. Even there Turkish Administration was comparatively ineffective. A political officer of the British Expeditionary Forces who worked in the marsh region during and after the First World War gives a picture of the Turkish administration in this part of Iraq during its last days.[2]

> There was control in the towns, a light hand on the surrounding tribes, a faint supervision often vanishing altogether among remote Marsh Arabs. Thus my own immediate post-war district of the Middle Gharraf (the ancient Lagash), midway between Tigris and Euphrates, had ceased to be administered by the Turks ten years before the War because of their inability to collect revenues, and three of my Turkish predecessors, who were too intent on revenue collection, had been murdered.

Like the rest of the marsh region, ech-Chibayish remained cut off from the outside world during the Ottoman occupation. There was no government agent in the village till 1893, and the only authority recognized throughout the whole region was that of the shaikh.

For the previous seven centuries all the tribesmen of Iraq had lived under feudal shaikhdoms. During the Ottoman domination, hardship and insecurity throughout the country grew owing to the destruction of irrigation works, lack of communications and the absence of any organized administration. With this lack of law and order there was a constant state of hostility among the tribes, which strengthened feudalism and deepened its roots. To all this, Beni Isad were no exception. Their shaikhs ruled

[1] *Wali* = governor-general of a Turkish *vilayet*.
[2] Bertram Thomas, *The Arabs*, London, 1937, p. 287.

despotically over their followers as landowners, military commanders and judges.

Though his lands were in theory leased from the Wali, to whom dues were supposed to be paid, the shaikh in practice held land without permission and paid no dues on it. Nor were there fixed boundaries to his lands; everything depended on how far he could push away his neighbours by force and use land which was neither his nor theirs. He allocated land to his followers arbitrarily, according to his personal wishes. They cultivated for him, and though there were supposed to be rules and principles governing crop division—usually one-third for the shaikh and the rest for the cultivator—it was subject to the shaikh's whim; if he confiscated the whole crop, the cultivator had no redress. There were many other dues: the 2½ rupees (187 *fils*) due on every 100 mats, called *sas il-bowari* (the dues of mats); the 2½ *qran*[1] (47 *fils*) due annually on each buffalo, called *koda*; and the date-palm due which varied from 2½ *qran* (46 *fils*) to one rupee (75 *fils*) from year to year, again according to the whim of the shaikh. The shaikh also confiscated the rifle of every tribesman who used it inside the tribe in a quarrel, and imposed fines on those of his followers who caused disorder. If a member of the tribe were killed, the shaikh received the compensation, took the half which was supposed by custom to be given to the murdered man's family and left the family to share the remaining half equally with all the tribe. Marriages of tribesmen were arranged by him, or at least required his approval, and thus, if he desired, he could take a portion of the brideprice. When the shaikh wished to go to Baghdad or Basra or when he found brides for his sons or brothers, each clan of the tribe was expected to contribute.

The shaikh could take land from any of his followers and give it to another. He might banish any tribesmen from his territory. Those who disobeyed him had their huts burnt, their cattle and belongings plundered. If a tribesman found that the shaikh did not wish him to live on his territory, or if he had been on bad terms with him, he could only move away from the shaikh's district, often taking his kinsmen with him.

The executive power of the shaikh was administered by the *mukhtār*[2] or clan heads, by members of the ruling clan, especially the Shaikh's own sons and brothers, and by his slaves. The clan heads had no power of their own. They were instruments of the shaikh, passed on his orders and collected his dues and fines. If they were greatly feared among the tribesmen it was only because they were acting for the shaikh. Members of the Ahl Khayūn clan, the ruling clan of the Beni Isad tribe, used to enjoy great authority. They held various offices under the shaikh and were his representatives in the distant parts of the region. The shaikh's slaves acted as a police force and messengers and some were made agents and even deputies.

---

[1] *Qran* is an Indian unit of money, equals 19 *fils* or 4½ pence.
[2] The chiefs of the clans were called *mukhtārs* and not *ṣirkals* during the days of the shaikhdom.

Judicial authority was vested in the shaikh. Jurisdiction was based on the *sowani* (the traditional tribal law). In simple cases the shaikh used to pronounce his judgments alone. If, however, the case were complicated, he summoned some of the notables (*ajawid it-tayfa*), especially those who had sound knowledge of the tribal law, and presided over them in council. Such a council had only an advisory power—decisions always resting with the shaikh himself.

In short, the Ahl Khayūn were a military aristocracy who led the Beni Isad in their many tribal wars. During a period of about 240 years, between the Beni Isad's migration to the ech-Chibayish region and the establishment of an external administrative control in 1915, the tribe fought against all the other tribes of the district, against many tribes of the Amara and li-Hwaiza regions, and against the Ottoman army. Shaikh Khayūn, for example, led many expeditions into Amara and li-Hwaiza and lived in those districts for many years. His son, Shaikh Hasan, lived in his enemy's territory in il-Mijarra for five years. Later, he himself fled with the majority of Beni Isad to li-Hwaiza where they lived 11 years, after being defeated in a battle against the Ottoman army.

In all these long wars the tribe gained nothing but military glory, and lost a large number of its sons. The tribesman's views of the latter aspect of war were well reflected in a war song (*hosa*) which said: *chāna sahmi il-maw wil-firni il-ghairi?*, meaning literally: 'Then my share is the bullets while the sweet-meats are for the others?' It echoed an ambivalence in the attitude of warriors who had to suffer the casualties, while the chiefs and commanders enjoyed most of the prestige and the booty. The Beni Isad endured heavy losses and were reduced to poverty by repeated battles, military evacuations, and epidemics following their campaigns.

Although their normal political life was one of constant raiding and warfare, the Beni Isad accepted the military leadership of the Ahl Khayūn, endured the hardships of war, and pursued values of a warrior society. But when peace was finally imposed on the region, the people no longer depended for their very survival upon powerful military rulers and became more conscious of the harsher side of autocracy; whilst the rulers no longer depended on their people to further their military gains, and grew less careful of their welfare. This explains why the Beni Isad were so ready later to turn against the ruling clan of Ahl Khayūn.

THE BEGINNINGS OF CENTRAL CONTROL

From 1865 onwards the Turks paid increasing attention to the ech-Chibayish district; a few gendarmeries were established, one of them at Sūg ish-Shyūkh, which later became the headquarters of a *qaḍa* (subprovince). But even after Basra (to which ech-Chibayish was administratively attached) had became a separate *vilayet*, peace was far from being established in the district. In the Hor of ech-Chibayish, boats were frequently plundered and travellers needed the protection of the shaikh.

Even Turkish army officers and government officials travelled with a guard of the shaikh's men and were delivered from one Turkish post to another against receipts.[1]

As part of their new policy the Turks sought to induce the tribes to settle and cultivate and their shaikhs to become Turkish officials. Some of the powerful shaikhs were accordingly appointed administrative officers. Under Midhat Pasha, Wali of Baghdad (1869-1872), Nasir Pasha Ahl Sadūn, the paramount shaikh of the il-Mintifig tribal confederation in il-Mintifig province, 'became the Pasha's chosen and willing tool to tame the Muntafig'.[2] Then Nasir Pasha was appointed *mutasarrif* (governor) of Basra and Shaikh Mihyi Ahl Khayūn of Sūg ish-Shyūkh Qaḍa.

Mihyi was the first shaikh of the Ahl Khayūn to co-operate with the Turks. After him, his brother Shaikh Hasan Ahl Khayūn worked with Nasir Pasha Ahl Sadūn, the *mutasarrif* of Basra at that time, in administering the tribal district of ech-Chibayish, and this co-operation resulted in one of the most useful projects in the district, namely, a dam from Sūg ish-Shyūkh to il-Gurna, Sadat Nasir Pasha, which was built under Shaikh Hasan's supervision with the forced labour of thousands of tribesmen.

The partnership, however, was short-lived. The Khayūni shaikh soon rebelled against the authority of his *mutasarrif*, and, after destroying the great dam which he himself had helped to build, found himself confronted by an Ottoman punitive expedition.

When Shaikh Hasan had been defeated by the government forces and fled over the Persian border to li-Hwaiza, a large number of Beni Isad followed him. But when the Beni Turuf—the Persian Marsh Dwellers—cut off the water from their fields, they found life so hard that many began to return to ech-Chibayish.

In the village, meanwhile, the Wali established a gendarmerie and a military telegraph office. He appointed Chayid Ahl Khayūn, a nephew of the defeated Hasan, as shaikh and gave him command of a detachment of local native police stationed in the vicinity. During this period, the Ottoman adminstrative centre was at il-Hammar village.

Despite these moves towards central control, conditions in ech-Chibayish grew worse. Members of the Ahl Khayūn often crossed the marsh from li-Hwaiza to plunder and kill; and such was the state of anarchy that in 1896 Shaikh Chayid was imprisoned for failure to keep order. Even the appointment of a resident *mudīr* (administrative officer) did little at first to improve the situation.

[1] Qais Ahl Khayūn showed me one of these receipts. It was dated (29 Rabi'a il-Awwal, 1314 A.H.) (A.D. 1896) and addressed to Shaikh Jnah Ahl Kihyi Ahl Khayūn who was at that time acting for Shaikh Chayid Ahl Mhammad Ahl Khayūn who was absent in Baghdad. The receipt acknowledged the 'safe' arrival of a Turkish army captain at the Turkish post at Hammar Beni Htait.

[2] H. S. Longrigg, op. cit., p. 308.

After the deposition of Chayid, the shaikhdom remained vacant for some time, due to the struggle for power among the Ahl Khayūn themselves, especially among Shaikh Hasan's sons. For Hasan, now old, crippled and poor, abandoned all hope of regaining power and left the matter to his 19 sons. Eventually, in 1904, Salim Ahl Khayūn, the seventeenth son, succeeded in getting himself appointed to the rulership by sheer force of ability and ambition, despite a longstanding feud with the Wali of Basra. But although he showed extraordinary ability in holding the shaikhdom in the face of his elder brothers' claims, the dynastic struggle was by no means over. On many occasions the smouldering fire of the bitter fight for power burst into flames—resulting once in a fierce shooting match among six of the shaikh's brothers, which ended in the deaths of all the contestants. Indeed, Salim only kept his central political role at the cost of giving his brothers a free hand in the village—a policy whose results greatly added to the people's grievances.

Nevertheless, his conduct of government at ech-Chibayish made sufficient impression on the Turks to induce them to transfer their administrative centre back from ech-Chibayish to il-Hammar, reducing the former from a *qaḍā* to a *nāḥiya*.[1] The shaikh, in fact, adopted a strong pro-Ottoman policy, and through his energy and personality, restored some degree of law and order. He maintained good relations with the administrative officers at il-Hammar, but completely dominated them. He was also appointed captain of the police stationed at ech-Chibayish.

Unfortunately, the pro-Ottoman tendencies which at first so strengthened Shaikh Salim's position were later to bring about the end of the Khayūni ru'le over Beni Isad. In 1914 his allegiance to the Turks made him a marked man for the British Expeditionary Force which invaded Basra *vilayet*. Sparing no efforts to capture him, they took him prisoner at ech-Chibayish in December, later sending him as a prisoner of war to India. Shaikh Salim was allowed to return from India in 1919. Upon his arrival at ech-Chibayish, he again assumed control of the Beni Isad.

In 1919 the tribes of ech-Chibayish, Beni Htait, Abada, Beni Musharraf and Ahl Hisan were all attached to Sūg ish-Shyūkh District under Shaikh Salim Ahl Khayūn as *mudir* and the Political Officer reported 'there has not been a single hitch in the administration to date'.[2]

Shaikh Salim occupied himself with new intrigues, instead of concentrating on tribal affairs in an attempt to regain confidence. As he had been a member of the Constituent Assembly and a Minister-without-Portfolio in the interim Iraqi government, he found it too degrading to obey administrative officers and began a campaign of disobedience, inciting neighbouring tribes to defy the new government. He 'had come to be regarded as paramount shaikh over the whole of the Hammar Lake and as far east

---

[1] *Qaḍā* is a unit at the penultimate level in Iraqi local administration; *nāḥiya* is a unit at the lowest level.

[2] *Administrative Reports of the Muntafiq Division.*

as the boundary of the Basra *liwa*. He farmed the more important government taxes, entirely dominated the government representative, the *mudīr* of Chabaish, and paid no attention to the orders of the *mutasarrif*.[1] The government tried to avoid taking any military action against him, but he disregarded their warnings and refused to meet the governor of the province or to pay his land dues. After showing considerable patience, the government were obliged to take action. Early in December 1924 an ultimatum dropped from the air by planes stated that 'Owing to the disobedience of Shaikh Salim Ahl Khayūn, ech-Chibayish village will be destroyed from the air to-morrow and the Ahl ech-Chibayish will have to leave it'. The planes bombed the shaikh's guest house and homestead and both were burned down. The shaikh, his brothers and cousins fled and the police and army destroyed his mud fortresses near ech-Chibayish. A strong police post was established at ech-Chibayish itself on the site of the shaikh's guest house. Shaikh Salim took refuge in the Hor, hoping in vain for the support of the Beni Isad whom he and his forefathers used to lead to war. He tried to organize bands in the Hor to cut communications and resist the government, but for the first time in his life, and indeed in all the history of Ahl Khayūn, an elder had the courage to state clearly and boldly 'To-day the tribe is not with you. You left them to your brothers who ruined them. Nobody has remained loyal to you or to your brothers. You had better save your own life.' Later Salim and his brother Ghadhban were arrested. Both were taken to Basra for trial. Salim was sentenced to three years' imprisonment, and his brother to ten months. Shaikh Salim was sent to Mosul[2] prison. Imprisonment was then commuted into compulsory residence in Mosul itself, and on 26 April 1927 he was allowed to live in Baghdad. Later, however, when his brother Ghadhban went to live as an outlaw in the Hor, Shaikh Salim was brought back to Mosul. In April 1930 the restriction of residence was lifted again, except for the three southern Provinces, Basra, Amara and il-Mintifig. At the beginning of 1931 the government granted Shaikh Salim 9,151 acres of rich land at Kanān in Dyala Province near Baghdad, and he chose to live on his new estate.

ADMINISTRATION WITHOUT THE SHAIKHS

When Shaikh Salim was arrested, the main aims of government policy were to abolish the shaikhdom of Beni Isad altogether, and to establish a strong administrative control over ech-Chibayish, using the clan heads as government representatives. It was hoped that members of Ahl Khayūn, the former noble clan, would become loyal citizens with no special privileges.

Until 1924, ech-Chibayish was without any government agent, the centre

[1] *Report by His Britannic Majesty's Government to the Council of the League of Nations on the Administration of Iraq for the year 1925,* Colonial Office, London, 1926, p. 34.
[2] The most northerly Province in the country.

of the administrative unit being at il-Hammar, a village some ten miles to the west. When Shaikh Salim fled from ech-Chibayish, strong contingents of police took control of the village. Later the government not only transferred the centre of administration from il-Hammar to ech-Chibayish, but also changed it from a *nāḥiya* to a *qayimmaqamiya*[1] and an administrative officer, *qāyimmaqām*, with a staff, was appointed. This was a necessary measure to meet the new situation arising from the abolition of the shaikhdom, as the district now required stronger and more efficient administrative control. When by 1929 order was restored and the new regime was well established, ech-Chibayish was again converted into a *nāḥiya* and was attached to Sūg ish-Shyūkh *qaḍā*.

Under the new system, the clan heads, who had been called *mukhtār* and acted on behalf of the shaikh, were installed as *ṣirkals* after they had been clearly shown their duties under the new regime. Every officially recognized clan head was allowed to choose the headman of each lineage in his clan as a *mukhtār* to help him in carrying out the government's orders. All the lands which had been under Shaikh Salim's control were registered in the names of the clan heads. Each received the land which his clan had actually been using at the time.

The new regime is based on direct rule through the clan heads. In legal disputes the tribesmen can go to the government which deals with them according to a system of law in force over all the country. In certain cases, such as murder or elopement, the tribesmen can ask that the case be heard under 'The Tribal Criminal and Civil Disputes Regulations'.[2] In such disputes judgment is effected by councils of arbitrators elected by the contesting parties and sentences are passed by the Administrative Officer according to the recommendation of these councils. The tribesmen are free to settle minor disputes through the clan heads, but they can always go to the government house in the village for judgment. The clan heads, on the other hand, may not deal with any major case, such as murder, without informing the Administrative Officer in the village.

Land holding is now controlled by the government and any land problem, however unimportant, is supposed to be dealt with and settled by government officers, not by the clan heads. Thus the new regime gives the clan heads no scope for exploitation.[3]

[1] The administrative units in Iraq are *mutaṣarrif*, each of which is composed of a number of *qayimmaqamiya*, each governed by a *qāyimmaqām*, and composed of a number of *nāḥiyas*, each governed by a *mudír nāḥiya*.
[2] The Tribal Criminal and Civil Disputes Regulation was enacted on 27 July 1918 by the Mesopotamian Expeditionary Force to 'arrange for the speedy settlement of disputes whether of a civil or criminal nature between tribesmen, in accordance with tribal customs'. These regulations were enforced against tribesmen, defined in the Regulation as 'members of a generally recognized tribe or tribal section which has been accustomed to settle its disputes by recourse to the arbitration of elders or shaikhs and not by recourse to the courts of the land as ordinarily constituted'.
[3] For details about land tenure see Chapter 8.

THE ṢIRKAL AND THE MUKHTĀR

The office of *ṣirkal* is the only important traditional political office which has been retained under the new regime. The *ṣirkal* is appointed and removed by the Governor of the Province (*il-mutaṣarrif*) according to the recommendation of the Administrative Officer (*mudīr in-nāḥiya*) of ech-Chibayish, and with the approval of the Minister of the Interior in Baghdad. In choosing a *ṣirkal*, hereditary and selective principles are combined. According to the rule of primogeniture, very important in native life, the eldest son of the *ṣirkal* is his preferred successor. But the administrative officer does not recommend such a son without making sure that he possesses certain personal qualifications, including popularity and sound judgment. A newly-appointed *ṣirkal* must guarantee to perform his duties faithfully and to pay government dues. He undertakes to be held responsible for any disobedience or disorder among his clan and to inform the government of any crime or offence which takes place within his territory.

When a *ṣirkal* dies leaving a son who is a minor, and the elders of the clan want the latter to take over his father's position in the absence of a suitable adult successor, a father's brother or father's brother's son of the boy or, if there is no such kinsman, a *khayir* (man of good fame), may be appointed to fill the post till he attains manhood.

If a *ṣirkal* abuses his office and fails to carry out government orders he can be dismissed at the request of the Administrative Officer. If the *ṣirkal* exploits his clansmen or maltreats them, a number of their elders and notables can submit a petition to the Administrative Officer. If a *ṣirkal* is held to have exceeded his authority, he can be checked and the dispute between him and his clansmen settled.

There is less formality in the appointment of the *mukhtār*, or lineage head, for he has no direct political connection with the government. In practice the *mukhtār* represents his lineage to the *ṣirkal*. Almost invariably, in every lineage the eldest adult male is the *mukhtār*, unless such an elder is already unpopular with his tribesmen. By virtue of his seniority and his headship of a large kin group within his lineage, the eldest man of the lineage enjoys the highest prestige and authority, and the *ṣirkal* naturally refers to him in every matter concerning his lineage. If a *mukhtār* dies, the next man recognized by his lineage as having authority automatically succeeds him.

The *ṣirkal* is required to maintain law and order among his followers by settling all minor offences in accordance with tribal law and referring major cases to the government. He is expected to pay all government dues, which consist mainly of land tax. He organizes all communal labour which may be demanded from his clan by the government. He sees that outlaws, fugitives and military conscripts are handed over to the appropriate government authority.

Towards his clan the *ṣirkal* has great responsibilities, as clansmen refer

to him in all their troubles and difficulties. He is regarded not merely as
political head of the clan, but as a patron and guardian. He must settle clan
disputes either by personal intervention, through the councillors of his
clan, or through the government, in which case he is responsible for carrying the matter through to a final conclusion.

He is expected to represent his clan and faithfully express their views
and wishes to the government. He must try to get the local administration
to grant their requests. In disputes between his clan and other clans he
must act as representative of his clan and he must defend their interests.
He should maintain a guest house in which his clansmen can meet, rest
and discuss matters of interest or moment. He is expected to be hospitable
on all occasions and play a major part in clan feasts; to help all the poor
members of his clan by loans and gifts of money and crops, and by concessions of crops or land.

The *şirkal* has also certain social and economic rights and privileges.
His followers must obey and respect him as a chief and political head. He
has the right to intervene in their disputes and settle them according to the
tribal traditions and law or to refer them to the government of the village.
His intervention in private matters such as betrothals, compensation, or
any similar matters is highly respected and his wishes usually complied
with. He has a one-third share of crops from all the cultivated land he
controls. He has the right to sell for his own profit all the grass which grows
on the uncultivated land within his territory.[1] Some *şirkals* exact dues on
fishing expeditions and migrant labourers.

A *mukhtār* has only the obligation of an ordinary villager towards the
government. He acts as a liaison officer between his lineage and the *şirkal*.
He looks after the affairs of his lineage and helps the *şirkal* in any matter
concerning his own lineage. He has the same social prerogatives among his
own lineage as the *şirkal* among his clan, but does not hold the equivalent
of the *şirkal's* economic rights, or the right to settle disputes.

Each clan has at least one *şirkal*. Ahl Ghrīj and il-Hadadiyīn clans, the
second and third in size, have respectively four and three *şirkals* each,
since in their case the government was unwilling to trust a single man with
such large followings and substantial land resources. However, the largest
clan, Ahl ish-Shaikh, has been left in the care of a single *şirkal*, Abdil-Hadi
Ahl Khayūn, a man of considerable prestige. Ahl Khatir is the only other
clan which is headed by a Khayūni *şirkal*.

Thaban Ahl Khayūn, the only living son of Shaikh Salim Ahl Khayūn,
has a unique position in the village. His father wanted him to become an
afandi,[2] and gave him the best education available in the country. Though

---

[1] This is only in the case of some *şirkals* who hold lands beyond the southern
edge of Hor il-Hammar which are covered by grass in the season of low water.
The right of grazing, called '*shat marta*" is bought by shepherd tribes who come to
the region for this purpose.

[2] A term now applied to any literate man wearing European clothes and belong-
ing to the townspeople.

Thaban graduated in the Faculty of Law of Baghdad, he has always been attached to ech-Chibayish and its tribal life. At the age of eleven, he witnessed the destruction of his father's shaikhdom and the distribution of his land and power. In the succeeding years he saw him tried, imprisoned and exiled. Being the only living son of his father, he has always dreamed of becoming the Shaikh of Beni Isad. Since he came to live permanently at ech-Chibayish in 1945 he has worked hard, first to attain authority and power and then to acquire the lost lands and the shaikhdom. In the beginning he relied largely upon political agitation and when this proved fruitless, he tried to buy or reclaim patches of land. He courts popularity among the people by every possible means—feasts, gifts, and help through his friends in the government. He has built a new and ostentatious guest house and keeps up the old Shaikh's custom of serving coffee every morning. He intervenes in every tribal matter and calls himself 'Shaikh Thaban'.

In fact Thaban is not a shaikh nor even a ṣirkal. His few patches of land do not confer on him any political power. The villagers appreciate his help but never look upon him as a man of any political authority. They respect him because he is Shaikh Salim's son, but they know well that the time of the shaikhdom has passed. The Administrative Officer always checks Thaban's activities. With the help of his cousin, Habīb Ahl Khayūn, he has succeeded in creating a small group of supporters, but since both the people of ech-Chibayish and the government are aware of their aims, their efforts are not likely to prove successful.

Ahl ish-Shaikh clan used to be most closely associated with the Shaikh and Ahl Khayūn, the noble clan. It was formerly governed directly by the shaikh and thus had no clan head. When the government installed the clan heads as ṣirkals they had to choose a ṣirkal for the large and powerful clan of Ahl ish-Shaikh. It was not practical to choose a clansman for this post as there was no-one who could command the respect of the entire clan and impose order upon it. At that critical period only a Khayūni might rule the clan as Ahl ish-Shaikh would only recognize the authority of Ahl Khayūn. The whole matter depended on choosing the right Khayūni man.

The government did not hesistate to choose Abdil Hadi Ahl Khayūn, a nephew of Shaikh Salim. He was chosen to take over after the defeat of Shaikh Salim in his campaign of disobedience against the government, just as his own father, Chayid Ahl Khayūn, had been chosen to rule over Beni Isad after Shaikh Hasan Ahl Khayūn, Salim's father, had been defeated in his war with the Ottoman army.

Abdil Hadi Ahl Khayūn succeeded in a policy of co-operating with the government and peace and order were restored. He proved to be a new type of Khayūni who did his utmost for the tribesmen at the expense of his private interests. He gradually secured the devotion of the whole tribe. The other ṣirkals of the village began to ask his advice in important matters, especially those which concerned problems outside their clans. Gradually, he came to be looked upon as a sort of general ṣirkal of the tribe or head chief of the village. The government put full confidence in him and was pleased to watch the tribe rally around him. Thus he united in himself two seemingly incompatible attitudes, loyalty to tribal leadership and loyalty to the State.

One of the features of the tribe's political life during the days of the old shaikhdom was the tribal councils. They were of two types. First there was *amra* (the war assembly) composed of all members of the tribe who were capable of bearing arms. This type of council was held to prepare for war and to discuss military plans if there were a threat of war. Secondly there was the council of *ajawid it-tayfa* composed only of *ajawid* (worthies), which was held to consider matters of general importance or to create a new rule in tribal law. Such councils were summoned by the Shaikh, held at his guest house, and presided over by him. They were only advisory, as all decisions rested with the shaikh. Under the new regime, there is no question of war councils, but the need for councils of worthies still arises from time to time. On such occasions the tribe always look to Abdil Hadi Ahl Khayūn, because he has the strongest personality in the village and he is the only clan head who enjoys the confidence of both the tribe and the government.

Abdil-Hadi's guest house is considered to be the guest house not only of Ahl ish-Shaikh clan but of the whole tribe. As in the guest houses of the old shaikhs, coffee is served every morning. In any matter of general concern, the Administrative Officer consults Abdil-Hadi and seeks his advice. He is the only clan head who has two seals,[1] the first being his seal as a *şirkal* of Ahl ish-Shaikh clan, and the other, which Abdil-Hadi calls *il-muhur ich-chibīr* (the big seal) his seal as a *şirkal* of ech-Chibayish. In cases concerning his clan followers he uses the seal of the office of *şirkal*, but in cases of other members of the tribe he uses the big seal.

It must, however, be stressed that, though Abdil Hadi-Ahl Khayūn has influence over all the clans of the village, he never exceeds his authority, nor does he abuse his strong political position. He neither interferes in the affairs of the other *şirkals*, nor tries to further his personal interests through his authority and power. He has no ambition to be a shaikh or to rule over the whole tribe.

Political Changes, Movements and Economic Life of Beni Isad since their Migration to Iraq in the Seventh Century

STAGE I: Seventh to Thirteenth Centuries

   Political Changes: Under the Islamic empires until the fall of the Abbasid Empire in 1258 A.D.

   Residence: Between Basra and Hit on the Euphrates and Wasit on the Tigris, mainly in Basra, Kufa and il-Qadisiya districts.

   Economic Life: Camel-herding and agriculture.

---

[1] Every *şirkal* of the village has a seal (*muhur*) bearing his name and title.

STAGE 2: Thirteenth Century—c.1760

Political Changes: Islamic emirates under princes, with an organized army, till defeated by Ahl Sadūn tribal federation.

Residence: The Middle Euphrates region, especially il-Hilla district.

Economic Life: Agriculture.

STAGE 3: c.1760-1893

Political Changes: Military feudal shaikdom, highly centralized, wars, emergence of Ahl Khayūn as an effective political power, assimilation of great number of local tribal segments, Shaikh Hasan's defeat and flight to li-Hwaiza in Persia. Total destruction of tribal army.

Residence: Roaming widely in the marsh region of Iraq and Persia from Beni Saīd to il-Midina and from the southern edge of Hor il-Hammar to li-Hwaiza with il-Isawi first and then ech-Chibayish as headquarters.

Economic Life: Plunder, crop-raiding in the marshes with intensive agriculture in il-Isawi district.

STAGE 4: 1893-1924

Political Changes: Feudal shaikhdom under Shaikh Salim and others with ineffective Turkish, British and Iraqi administration. Abolition of shaikhdom in 1924.

Residence: Settled in ech-Chibayish after losing il-Isawi and other agricultural land which they used to cultivate.

Economic Life: Mat-weaving learned from Ma'dan, summer and winter agriculture until excessive flooding. Cattle-keeping and labour migration to il-Garraf region only.

STAGE 5: 1924 till the present day

Political Changes: Administration under the Iraqi Government. Strong administrative centre. Division of power and lands among the chiefs of the clans.

Residence: Settled in ech-Chibayish.

Economic Life: Mat-weaving, cattle-keeping, occasional summer cultivation, labour migrations to il-Garraf, Basra and il-Hor for reed-gathering and fishing.

GOVERNMENT AT ECH-CHIBAYISH TO-DAY

Ech-Chibayish to-day is a *nāḥiya*, that is, the smallest administrative unit. Besides ech-Chibayish village, the *nāḥiya* also embraces the villages of il-Hammar and Li-Fhūd.[1]

The administrative officer and his clerk in ech-Chibayish village are responsible for the direction and management of all the activities of the *nāḥiya*. The administrative officer should maintain law and order, and settle the disputes which come within his authority, referring the others to the officers concerned. He collects the government's land and municipal

---

[1] See map opposite. The boundary of the *nāḥiya* runs from il-Kharfiya in the east to Ahl Ismaiyīl in the west and from il-Abid in the north to the railway line beyond Hor-il-Hammar in the south. The registered population of *nāḥiyat* ech-Chibayish according to the 1947 census is 29,231 and the important tribes living within its boundary are: Beni Isad Ahl Fartūs, Iddbat, Albu Ayish, Albu Shama, Beni Msharraf and Li-Fhūd.

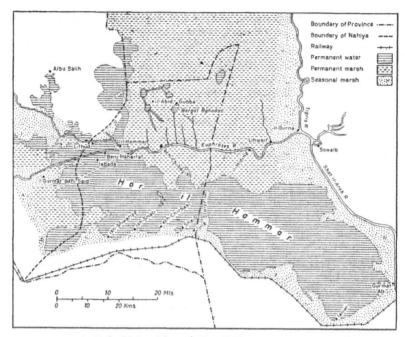

Ech-Chibayish and Hor il-Hammar region

taxes. He supervises the maintenance of the existing dykes and the building of new ones to save the villages and fields from floods. He is head of the village municipality and is responsible for all its functions and duties. All the officials of the village are directly responsible to him. The clerk acts as his secretary and sometimes deputizes for him.

The police force consists of one police officer, one police inspector and sixteen policemen.

There is a Municipal Council composed of six notables of the village,[1] elected for four years; half of them are replaced every two years. The council meets irregularly as the situation requires and deals with all municipal problems, reaching its decisions by voting. The council is headed by the administrative officer, and there are two clerks and six employees, including three night-watchmen to guard the village market, the government offices, and the houses of the in-Nahiya section of the village.

The council is responsible for the cleanliness and lighting of the village,

[1] It is important to note here the composition of this council, namely: five rich men, traders or shop owners, and one landholder. None of these people would have been chosen to sit on any traditionally constituted council; for their indulgence in commerce runs counter to all traditional values (cf. Chapter 12).

D

for fixing the prices of food-stuffs, such as fruit and fish, and the fares for water transport. It distributes a limited amount of financial assistance to the needy on certain occasions and pays fixed monthly salaries to fifteen persons in the village. The main projects it had carried out up to 1953 were a brick embankment along the in-Nahiya section of the village; a few modern houses built for the residence of some of the government officials; and two brick bridges at the ends of the embankment.

There is also a financial clerk who, aided by a number of messengers, collects taxes on cereal and other food-stuffs sold in the village. His office is under the control of the Ministry of Finance but his work is supervised by the administrative officer.

GOVERNMENT AUTHORITY AND PRESTIGE

When they first came under the direct rule of the government Ahl ech-Chibayish welcomed the new regime because of the hope it gave them of throwing off the yoke of corrupt despots and of enjoying justice and security. Their initial impression of government was that it gave much and took little, in striking contrast to the rule of Ahl Khayūn; they were also impressed by the display of strength in dealing with trouble-makers, and there was an excellent atmosphere for the building up of the new regime.

In addition to the general reasons which made Ahl ech-Chibayish welcome and support the new regime, the *sirkals* appreciated their new power and prestige. If the regime collapsed they would lose the lands they held and the authority they enjoyed. Their co-operation has been one of the chief factors making for the success of the government administration in ech-Chibayish. During the many crises through which the young administration has passed, such as the revolt of Sūg ish-Shyūkh in 1935, the long troubles caused by Ghadhban Ahl Khayūn, Shaikh Salim's brother, and later the three months' return of Shaikh Salim to ech-Chibayish in 1945, the *sirkals* gave the government active support.

When the government accomplished more than the people had expected, it won tremendous prestige. Officials performed their duties faithfully and without abuse, inspired by the constructive spirit which prevailed during the 1920's in the administration in the country generally. The imposition of peace, justice and security, and the establishment of public services such as the school, the dispensary, the municipality and the veterinary clinic, all increased the prestige of the government. The people, deeply impressed, began to describe the government as *rabb thāni* (a second God.)

But much of this initial prestige was lost during the 1930's and to a greater extent during the 1940's. During the last few years there has been not only loss of prestige, but active grievance against the government for the inadequacy of the administrative machinery and the corruption of village officials.

The police authority of the village is a crucial example of this corruption.

The police are known to take bribes, sometimes quite openly. This corruption has affected the tribesmen's readiness to carry out government orders, and in most cases has aroused their contempt. It is the duty of the police to prevent gambling in the village, at least in the coffee shops, yet recently one of the most active gambling centres in the village was the police inspector's house, where he induced villagers to come regularly and play with him. As a result, the police officer was in no position to prevent gambling in the coffee shops or elsewhere in the village. This strikes most people as particularly reprehensible, as gambling is prohibited in Islamic law.

Nevertheless, in spite of these defects the impact of government on ech-Chibayish has been considerable. It is important to stress that this impact has been all the stronger because of the abolition of the shaikhdom. A contrast may be made here with the Tigris marsh dwellers, who still have a strong feudal shaikhdom and upon whom the impact of government has been negligible.

In the field of law and order the government has accomplished a great deal. Blood feuds have been completely checked, since the government compels the wronged party in a dispute to resort to tribal courts, to accept compensation in money, and not to take any unlawful action. Compensation in women is not paid in disputes settled by the government, and since every tribesman can take his disputes to the government, payment of women in compensation has become optional, resorted to only when disputes are settled through the ṣirkals, and then only in certain cases such as elopement and adultery. It is frequently only agreed upon nominally and an equivalent in money substituted. Many other tribal customs which used to cause disturbances among Ahl ech-Chibayish have been banned by the government.

The tribesman of ech-Chibayish is to-day more conscious of the government than he is of his tribal authorities. There is no shaikh and the ṣirkals differ little from government officials. There are no wars in which the tribesman might be made to feel tribal solidarity. His son goes to the government school and he and his family go to the government dispensary. He can lodge complaints against his fellow tribesmen and even against his ṣirkal at the government house.

In other aspects of native life the impact has been no less strongly felt. On the economic side, the prevalence of order and the opening of communications has encouraged contact with the outside world. A commercial class of traders and shopkeepers, who have ventured to break the barriers of the tribal traditions, has emerged. Trade itself has encouraged contact with the neighbouring towns and thus helped to introduce many new elements of urban life. The introduction to the village of schooling, however elementary and inefficient, has resulted in creating a number of literate villagers and encouraging enrolment in the government service. Those who have no opportunity to continue their studies or serve in the government tend to take up trade and shopkeeping or other similar jobs rather than mat-weaving and cultivation.

Conditions in ech-Chibayish during the last years of the shaikhdom left the villagers particularly disposed to co-operate with a new regime which promised improved standards of living and an end to the old extortions. Unfortunately, however, this receptive atmosphere has somewhat cooled through three decades of administrative corruption; and progress has been less rapid than one might have predicted at the outset.

4

Tribe, Clan, Lineage and *Khowwan*

THE inhabitants of ech-Chibayish consider themselves members of a single tribe, the Beni Isad. The village population of about 11,000 is divided among nine clans, each of which contains a number of lineages. The nucleus of the tribe was the four clans who claimed descent from four brothers, themselves descendants of Isad, the founder of the tribe. Beside these four clans, the tribe embraced fragments of other tribes and clans conquered and adopted into it during the military campaign of the Beni Isad in the Euphrates marshes. While some of these fragments later claimed descent from Isad, others retained their own traditions of origin.

Beni Isad were, according to their tradition, a bedouin tribe which migrated from Arabia more than 13 centuries ago and established themselves in a number of localities before they were forced to retire to ech-Chibayish as a result of defeat by their neighbours. During this time and particularly when they were driven to the marsh, the bedouin Beni Isad adopted and affiliated many fragments of other tribes, some of whom were of bedouin and others of Ma'dan origin, and so increased their military power. Until the abolition of the shaikhdom in 1924, the tribe composed of these heterogeneous groups was a political and military unit under the authority and control of the shaikh.

As a political unit the tribe is practically non-existent to-day, having ceased to function as such after the abolition of the shaikhdom. All the clans are now independently governed by *sirkals* under the direct control of the central government; and as a result, some clans have isolated themselves and acted as independent entities in paying compensation and in other similar matters. Tribal wars, when the tribe formerly acted as a unit, are virtually unknown to-day. The only fighting which has taken place since the shaikhdom was abolished was a war between Beni Isad and Ahl Hisan tribe of Gurmat Beni Saïd, because of a land dispute in 1945. The government acted very quickly, crushed the movement, restored order, and punished both sides very severely. In this war all the component clans of the tribe in ech-Chibayish rose up as one man, and every adult male, including old men, hurried to the field of battle without regard to origin or affiliation, successfully stirred up by the ex-shaikh who was in the village at that time.

The meaning of the term tribe is now so vague in the minds of the people of ech-Chabiyish, especially those of the new generation, that there is a noticeable confusion between the terms 'ashīra (tribe) and ḥamūla (clan). They tend to speak of their ḥamūla as 'ashīra and divide it into clans, lineages and families. Besides the abolition of the shaikhdom, another factor contributed towards this disintegration.

Ahl Khayūn, the noble clan, anxious to increase their followers for military purposes, assimilated fragments of alien clans and tribes, Ma'dan and others, who later also became known as Beni Isad. As happens in many confederacies, these heterogenous accretions reasserted their independence when the need for a protective alliance and the constraint of a despotic authority disappeared. Even clans claiming common descent, however, have now largely lost their sense of unity, and some of the original Beni Isad (the Ahl Abbas clan) have left ech-Chibayish altogether.

THE CLAN (IL-ḤAMŪLA)

The political and territorial subdivisions of the tribe are its clans. There are nine clans of Beni Isad. They vary in size from 155 to 4,500 persons and enjoy different status according to their origin and size. The most esteemed are the four claiming descent from the four brothers, Shaikh, Anaisi, Wnais and Wais, the descendants of Isad. Among these four clans, the Ahl ish-Shaikh is the most respected and esteemed not only because it is the largest and most powerful, but because it has had close contact with the shaikhs of the tribe. The shaikhs used to consider Ahl ish-Shaikh as their retinue and appoint from among them their agents, servants and bodyguards. The power and strength of this clan has increased and so have its numbers as a result of having adopted many segments of other clans. The status of the remaining five clans who do not claim descent from Isad (Ahl Ghrīj, il-Hadadiyīn, Ahl Khatir, Beni Ashiri and Ahl Limabir) is a function partly of size, partly of origin and partly of the occupations of their members. Thus il-Hadadiyīn enjoys relatively high status because of its size, whilst the even larger Ahl Ghrīj has the lowest status of all because of the counterbalancing obscurity of its origin and the despised occupations of its members.[1]

Each clan is subdivided into agnatic lineages. As with clans in the tribe, we find a ranking of lineages in the clan; but whereas the rank of the clan depends also on factors such as origin and occupation, that of lineages depends principally on numbers.

Although all the members of a clan are ideologically united by the fiction of common descent, recruitment by birth is frequently supplemented by adoption, an institution strongly motivated by its usefulness as a means of improving clan or lineage status. Its importance for an understanding of the clan and lineage system demands that we give it detailed consideration.

[1] See Chapter 12.

The process of adoption into lineage or clan is formally recognized by the name *il-kitba*, and confers full rights and obligations of membership in the adopted group. Such adoption seems to have occurred on a large scale in the past, so that many of the present families, lineages and even clans of Beni Isad belonged originally to other groups. Individuals coming to reside among the tribe have also been widely adopted, and are treated with special care and respect because they are considered to be refugees or weak persons who have a right to protection.

In time of tribal wars many weak segments of tribes came to live under the protection of the powerful Beni Isad and were ultimately adopted into it. Since these affiliations took place long ago, and because foreign origin affects the prestige of the lineage or clan concerned, it is not easy now to distinguish between those who were adopted into the tribe and those of pure Beni Isad origin. Nevertheless, many lineages and even clans are known to be foreigners. Even in later years, however, especially after 1924, there has been considerable adoption of lineages and segments of lineages.

The usual reasons for leaving a clan and joining a new one are desire for more effective military protection, and disputes over land or compensation, the two latter being preponderant in more recent years. The search for greater protection usually leads people to seek adoption into a group of noted strength and influence; and it is significant that although no lineages of the Ahl ish-Shaikh clan have ever been adopted elsewhere, most lineages and families seeking to transfer their allegiance from other groups try to gain acceptance into Ahl ish-Shaikh. This is because the latter is the biggest and most powerful clan of Beni Isad.

The procedure of adoption is as follows: Members of the injured party go to the *ṣirkal* of the clan into which they wish to be received, explain their wishes and specify the lineage into which they desire to be adopted. The *ṣirkal* discusses the matter with the group's original clan and if no reconciliation can be arranged, the *ṣirkal* orders the head of the lineage which they have chosen to adopt them. Two copies of a document recording the adoption are drawn up by a literate tribesman, one for each party. This document is signed by members of the adopting lineage and by one or two witnesses. After signing the document of adoption, the names of the adult males of the new members are registered in the book of compensation payers, *daftar il-muwadi*.

The following is a literal translation of an adoption document of Albu Masūd of il-Hadadiyīn clan into Ahl Sawwad and Albu Zdew lineages of Ahl ish-Shaikh clan. Adoption here was with two lineages instead of one. This is due to the fact that these two lineages are very closely related to each other and act as one in matters such as adoption:

In the Name of God, the Compassionate, the Merciful.

Date: 12/4/1944
20/5/1364
Friday.

Yes,[1] we, whose names are registered below, members of Ahl Sawwad and Albu Zdew lineages, have recorded our names and included ourselves in the father's brotherhood with the members of Albu Masud; [names of fourteen men], agreeing to pay shares of compensation as they do in penalties inflicted on ourselves or on them, except in the case of *is-soda*[2] (from which may God protect us), which will be shouldered by the culprit alone. Apart from this, we are brothers. We have penned this correct document and made God and a group of the people present witnesses to it.

[Stamped with nineteen thumb-prints of the adult men of the two lineages.]

Witness   Witness
Abbas Ahl Khayūn   Sayyid Yasīn is-Sayyid Mhana[3]

Before leaving our discussion of this institution, it should be noted that the many incentives tending to encourage it are counterbalanced, first by the reluctance of any clan to relinquish one of its lineages or lineage segments, and second by the fact that the clan into which the deserting party seeks adoption does not readily accept it until assured that the original clan is unwilling to be reconciled with it.

All members of a clan, born or adopted, display complete solidarity in payment of compensation and disputes with other clans of the tribe. If a member dies, it is the responsibility of the clan to help the family of the deceased either by subscribing to collect a sufficient sum of money to transfer the corpse to the holy city of in-Najaf, or by offering food on behalf of the bereaved family to all those who come to offer their condolences. If the family takes the usual course and decides to transfer the corpse itself, the whole clan divides into three sections, each of which shoulders the expenses for one of the three-day mourning ceremonies. While attending the mourning ceremonies, all families of the clan, as well as those of other clans who maintain friendly relationships with the deceased or with one of the members of his family, must offer gifts, usually of coffee or cigarettes, which cost between 250 and 750 *fils*. Those who are able, offer a sheep, which costs about ID 3/000.

THE LINEAGE[4]

Membership of a particular lineage is a significant index of a man's status in the community. The effective members of a lineage are heads of families.

[1] It is customary in documents of this kind written by natives to begin, quite unnecesarily, with the word 'na'am' (yes).   [2] See below, p. 51.

[3] Important documents such as this are usually signed by a Khayūni (a member of Ahl Khayūn noble clan) or *sayyid* (supposed descendant of the Prophet) or both, as witnesses.

[4] The lineage is given more than one name. Beside '*il-fakhiḍ*' (the thigh) it is often called *laḥama* (flesh) or *kishba* (wood). The bedouin gives names of parts of the human body, such as *baṭn* (belly), *fakhiḍ* (thigh) etc., to segments of the tribe.

The lineage is composed of all the descendants, men and women, who can trace their relationship in the male line to each other and to their ancestor some six or seven generations back. There are one or two lineages which have a depth of only four generations. As a result of adoption a lineage may contain individuals or whole families of other descent, in addition to the descendants of the supposed founder of the lineage.

There are 39 lineages in ech-Chibayish varying in size from 50 to 200 members. Apart from other factors, the size of a lineage depends on the number of strangers or non-lineage families adopted into it. Some of the bigger lineages are segmented into sub-lineages, each of which is supposed to be descended from a son of the lineage founder. Others have no internal structure relating the various families of which they are composed.

Lineages are normally territorially distinct from each other. Their members usually occupy adjacent islands, and hold one or more nearby patches of land, but territorial rights are vested in the clans, not in their component lineages. The majority of lineages in a given clan live together in a single territorial bloc; but a lineage will occasionally leave this bloc and acquire the right to live in the territory of another clan. In most cases the lineage seeking rights of residence in the territory of another clan has to be formally adopted into the clan of its hosts.

In ech-Chibayish there are four lineages living in the territory of clans to which they were not affiliated by origin or adoption. Their reasons for remaining unaffiliated reflect the relative prestige of the different clans:

Albu Masūd who had been originally of il-Hadadiyīn clan and later were adopted into Ahl ish-Shaikh clan in 1947, but live in Ahl Wnais clan territory;

Albu Zahrūn, who are of the Ahl ish-Shaikh clan, but live in Ahl Anaisi clan territory;

il-Bukhatra, who are of the Ahl ish-Shaikh clan, but live separately near Ahl Limabir;

Ahl Hajwal, who are of the il-Hadadiyīn clan, live with Ahl Khatir clan.

Three of these four lineages are of Ahl ish-Shaikh clan who, because of the high prestige of their clan, never change their affiliation; rather, others seek adoption into their clan. The fourth lineage lives in the territory of Ahl Khatir clan, who are of despised Ma'dan origin, a clan, therefore, into which none of Beni Isad would consent to be adopted.

These movements of lineages and sub-lineages may be due to the growth of the lineage itself, or to disputes and quarrels between the elders. By and large, however, the scarcity of dwelling islands restricts mobility, and, by confining lineages to their original residence, counteracts the tendency to fission. The dissenting group will often be forced to continue to live among the main body of its clansmen so that the chances of reconciliation after disputes are strong.

Strong solidarity unites members of the lineage, whose members often describe themselves as 'brothers', or 'father's brother's sons'. The term *'ammi* (my father's brother), is applied beyond the context of the family to all male members of the lineage in the father's generation. Respect and affection are expressed for women, young men and girls of the lineage, as towards mothers, brothers and sisters. Any insult, injury or harm befalling any member of the lineage is felt personally by every member. The lineage acts as a unit in external relations such as disputes, compensations and communal work. In disputes with members of other lineages, every member of the lineage feels as much involved in the case as the men concerned. All members of the lineage support their kin in disputes even if they are the aggressors, though the elders of the lineage may blame them in private.

Members of the lineage shoulder the compensation[1] for any crime committed by a lineage member against a member of any of the other lineages of the same clan. Besides this, the lineage has to contribute with other lineages of its clan to compensation for crimes committed by clansmen against members of other clans of the tribe, though there are certain crimes against other clans for which the guilty lineage has to shoulder sole responsibility.

Communal work is another occasion where the unity of the lineage is expressed. If the lineage is required to contribute labour to clan or administrative projects, its members always act as a united group *vis-à-vis* members of other lineages. In building a guest house for the chief of a clan, for instance, each lineage takes a part of the guest house, usually one pair of pillars, and competes with other lineages in trying to finish it first and best. On one occasion the Administrative Officer asked men of one of the lineages of Ahl ish-Shaikh clan to erect a reed weir across the Lughmaija stream. They refused to do the work and the Administrative Officer took a number of them into custody. After a few hours every adult male member of the lineage who happened to be in the village at the time went to the government house and begged the Administrative Officer either to release the men or to take them all into custody together. In their argument they stated clearly and repeatedly, 'Why should these four members shoulder alone the responsibility which rests equally with every one of us? We are one flesh (*laḥama wiḥda*).'

In internal matters, particularly marriage, the unity of the lineage is obvious and co-operation among its members is strong and effective. Marriages of members of the lineage are controlled by the lineage elders, especially when it is a question of girls marrying outside the lineage. A man has a strong obligation to marry his father's brother's daughter and only if the father's brothers happen to be without marriageable daughters is he supposed to seek a bride among other families of his own lineage. If it should happen that there are no girls of marriagable age in the lineage, he is expected to extend his search for a bride among his own clan. Only

[1] For a discussion of compensation see below, pp. 51–4.

if he cannot find a bride in his own clan may he look for one among other clans of the tribe. A low proportion of marriages takes place outside the clan, and only about 50 per cent of marriages are outside the lineage. In the sample of 120 families, 118 men were married to 164 wives. 63 (38.4%) of these wives were own father's brother's daughters, and 21 (12.8%) wives were lineage women other than father's brother's daughters. 84 (51·2%) of the 164 wives were thus lineage women. 18 (11%) were clanswomen and 33 (20·1%) were taken from other clans of the village. Only 29 wives (17·7%) were strangers to the village. Intra-lineage unions thus stand at 51·2%; intra-clan unions at 62·2%; and intra-tribal unions at 82·3%.

The Beni Isad claim that, in the past, the rule of endogamy was stricter than to-day. Long contact with non-bedouin cultures during their residence in various places in southern Iraq, long exile in Persia and in the eastern marshes after military evacuations by the Ottomans and finally 60 years of settled life in ech-Chibayish are responsible for this and many other changes in the old tribal culture.

Intra-lineage unions are very much encouraged by the custom of requiring a merely nominal brideprice in marriages between lineage members. While brideprice otherwise ranges from ID 50/000 to ID 100/000, intra-lineage brideprice is usually between ID 5/000 and ID 20/000. That of the Ahl Khayūn was ID 18/000, of the Ahl Hiji Sari and Albu Mkhaiwir, ID 14/000, while that of Ahl Awaiti was ID 7/000.

For the individual father the custom means that he accepts a low brideprice for his daughters, and balances this by being able to acquire wives for his sons at the same low rate, thus to some extent mitigating demands for sudden large capital outlays which in the ech-Chibayish economy are very hard to meet.

There is financial loss to those who have daughters only, or to those whose daughters outnumber their sons. Needy men sometimes venture to break the rule by giving their daughters in marriage outside the lineage. In doing so, they are making themselves liable to be treated as outsiders (as far as the brideprice is concerned), when they try to get wives for their sons from among their own lineage. Sometimes a man, even if his sons and daughters are equal in number, may have pressing debts or some urgent expenditure which he decides to meet with the very large sum of money he can obtain by marrying his daughter outside the lineage. He forgoes the advantage of a low brideprice for his son's marriage, consoling himself with the thought that he can delay his son's marriage indefinitely until more favourable economic conditions prevail.

There are other factors tending to strengthen the custom of marrying within the lineage. The first is that sons are not economically independent. Fathers, who control the family economy, are responsible for supplying the brideprice for their sons' marriages, and thus prefer girls of their own lineage whom they can get for a low brideprice. The second is that marriages with father's brother's daughters, or any other women of the lineage, are supposed to increase the chance of a successful marriage, since the bride is not a stranger in the family. A woman herself prefers to marry within her own lineage, because she fears ill-treatment if she marries into an outside group far from her kin; and some women even refuse extra-lineage marriage on the grounds that marriage inside their kin groups makes them less liable to be divorced or made second wives by further marriages.

Thirdly, since any male lineage member in the father's generation is looked upon as a father's brother and hence next in authority to the father, intra-lineage unions mean that men have their daughters married to others over whom they exercise considerable authority.

Any lineage man had the right to prohibit the marriage of any lineage girl to a man outside the lineage. The right, called *in-nahwa* (marriage prohibition), used to be a source of trouble. Lineage men asked for reparation if their rights were ignored and girls might be left unmarried for years, while, in a few cases, this right was misused in order to obtain money on relinquishing it. This right formerly allowed the prohibitor (*nāhi*) to kill any man who, in spite of his prohibition, dared to marry his potential lineage wife. If his prohibition was not heeded by his own kin, he might leave his lineage and demand his right. Usually a *nāhi* comes at night, fires a few shots in the air and shouts from a distance that he has come to proclaim his rights and that if these rights are not heeded he will come again soon to cause real harm or damage. The people concerned are supposed to form a delegation to soften his feelings; they must apologize and may sometimes offer presents of clothes to him. After a case 15 years ago, Ahl ech-Chibayish realized the abuses to which *in-nahwa* was open and Abdil Hadi Ahl Khayūn, the *ṣirkal* of Ahl ish-Shaikh clan, prohibited its practice among his clan and persuaded all the other clans of Beni Isad to do the same. They agreed and documents stating this prohibition were signed. Nevertheless, rights of *in-nahwa* are sometimes asserted, but neither the *ṣirkal* nor the government support them. The government takes strong measures, in the form of financial guarantees from those who attempt to prohibit the marriage of a lineage girl, and there is a tendency for the people to make written agreements between themselves to make sure that their kin cannot prohibit their daughters' marriages.

In marriage ceremonies, there is an obligation on the lineage to help the groom's father by subscriptions if he is a poor man, or by loans if the money required for the marriage is not available. In addition, every family of the lineage, as well as those of other lineages and clans with whom the groom's family has relations, must come to offer their congratulations and bring with them gifts of sugar, cigarettes or money. Such gifts correspond to the financial situation of the person who offers them, but usually cost between 150 and 500 *fils*. On the first morning of the marriage, closer friends of the groom's family must offer a gift of cooked food consisting usually of rice, chickens and so on, costing between 500 *fils* and ID 1/000.

These, together with the sugar, cigarettes and money gifts, are considered 'delayed debts', so that if a man is offered a gift of this kind, he must offer at least its equivalent at the earliest similar opportunity. They are very punctilious about the custom of offering gifts in such ceremonies, and those who fail to comply, especially if they are indebted, are open to strong disapproval. People do their utmost to meet such obligations, raising loans if necessary.

Members of the same lineage render one another valuable services in many other contexts. In projects which need a large number of men, such as building a guest house or a hut, it is usual to demand the help of lineage members. Unless one has strong reasons it is shameful not to comply with such a demand.

Being involved in the daily work of earning a living is never accepted as an excuse for refusing help and thus assistance causes temporary economic loss to those who have to offer it. Old men, widows and other needy members of the lineage have the right to ask younger members for help in difficult tasks such as bringing in fodder for their cattle; young members have strong moral obligations to comply with these requests. In the long run, however, compliance is also very much in one's own interests: for a lineage member who refuses help will not find anybody ready to come to his assistance, and there are no hired labourers in ech-Chibayish.

THE KHOWWAN

The lineage is a large unit, numbering sometimes as many as 200 members. Between the lineage and the family there is an intermediate unit of social organization, the *khowwan* (literally, 'brothers'). This is a group of men, each the head of a separate family, economically independent in earnings and household expenditure, but habitually acting as a single unit in matters concerning the marriages of their children and in paying compensation for certain crimes. They may be sons of one father, or they may have had a common grandfather. They generally inhabit neighbouring islands, or even the same island if space permits.

COMPENSATION: THE LEGAL ASPECT OF GROUP MEMBERSHIP

Il-faṣil is a compensation paid collectively by the culprit's family, lineage, clan or tribe, in women or money. It can be regarded as an index of unity, because in any crime, except those termed *is-soda* and *il-fasda* the penalty is shouldered by the whole Beni Isad collectively if the crime is committed against a member of another tribe, or by the culprit's own clan if it is committed against a member of another clan of the village. If the crime is committed within his own clan, it is the responsibility of his own lineage only.

Is-soda ('the black crime') includes adultery, elopement or attempted seduction. All these crimes are considered 'shameful'. In theory the culprit and his family alone shoulder the compensation, whether the crime is committed inside the clan, the tribe, or outside the village. In practice, however, the group of 'brothers' (*khowwan*) who hold corporate rights in each others' daughters and sisters, seldom leaves the culprit's family to bear the responsibility alone, though the offender may be left to himself if his group has previously warned him for other offences.

Similarly, *il-fasda* ('the bad crime') covers killing a chief or a fellow clansman, or stealing inside the village. Since these crimes are considered a threat to clan and tribal unity, the clan does not share in the payment of compensation for them.

The tribe has a written code called *sowani Beni Isad* in which there is a specific penalty for nearly every possible crime. Those crimes for which no penalties are specified are settled by creating new articles of the code at a special tribal council.

Except for minor crimes, compensation used to be paid in women only, but since the Marsh Dwellers were brought under the Iraqi administration in 1921, the central government has done its utmost to check this practice. Though many tribesmen still insist on being paid in women for major crimes, especially murder, they nevertheless realize the defects of this system.

Women given in compensation are taken in marriage by the plaintiff's family or kin. As they are taken from an enemy in compensation for a crime, it is believed that they are often ill-treated by their husbands and relatives-in-law.

The origin of this practice seems to be that, in the case of murder, the wronged party demanded a woman in compensation so that she might give birth to a child to replace the dead man. Thus, among some of the Marsh Dwellers of Amara, such women were allowed to return to their kin if they wished, after giving birth to a boy. On the other hand, the wronged party had the right to return the woman to her kin and claim another woman in her stead if she proved barren. Ahl ech-Chibayish say *lo abzerat fuselat* (she will have paid the penalty if she gives birth to a child), but in practice women do not return to their kin after bearing a child, nor are they exchanged if they prove to be barren.

Ahl ech-Chibayish hate giving their girls as compensation. If a woman of Ahl ech-Chibayish is maltreated by her kin or husband she says, 'Am I *fasliya* (a woman taken for compensation)?' But in spite of these sentiments and of the efforts of the administration, Ahl ech-Chibayish insist on having women in compensation for certain crimes, especially if such crimes, for example, elopement, have resulted in the loss to the injured group of a woman member.

The wronged party has the right to choose any woman or women from the culprit's group responsible for the payment. The father of the chosen woman demands the usual brideprice and the group concerned pay him, after making a collection among their members. If, however, in the case of *is-soda* crimes, the family does not include a marriageable girl, she may be chosen from the father's brothers' families.

Compensation among the Beni Isad varies greatly according to the crime. For example, that for killing a *ṣirkal* is four women or ID 150/000, and for killing a fellow-member of Beni Isad, two women or ID 75/000. For attempted seduction the compensation is ID 3/750 and for knocking out a tooth, 375 *fils* only.

When a crime is committed and the penalty fixed, the adult members of the lineage or clan whose names are recorded in the compensation book held by the lineage headman or the clan chief, pay equal shares to meet the penalty imposed. The culprit, in such cases, pays his share like any other member. As specified by Beni Isad, compensation payers are those who are capable of bearing arms. The usual age for a boy to be so considered is about sixteen, but boys who wish to have their names enrolled before that age are welcomed.

It is obvious that the smaller the group which has the responsibility for paying, the heavier the burden on its members. The shares in compensations for *is-soda* and *il-fasda* are especially heavy economic burdens. In a murder case which took place in April 1952 in Ahl ish-Shaikh clan, the lineage of the four accused men, Ahl Haji Sari, was ordered to pay about ID 600/000 as compensation, including costs of the case and of medical treatment for two persons who had been wounded. As Ahl Haji Sari lineage was composed of 32 adult males, the share of each adult was about ID 19/000. One or two families had to pay three shares, which came to ID 57/000. My paddler at ech-Chibayish was a member of this lineage and, with his eldest son, had to pay about ID 38/000, a sum which was totally beyond his means. He told me that he could only find this sum by selling his three cows and raising loans.

It might appear that the incidence of this financial responsibility would be offset by the gain to the group concerned when, in their turn, one of their members was the victim of an injury for which compensation had to be paid. However, according to the tribal law the compensation money must be divided into two halves, one to go to the family of the wronged man, the other to the larger group (lineage, clan or tribe) which would, if circumstances were reversed, be collectively responsible for paying compensation for a similar crime. This means that the responsibility for paying compensation is often more burdensome than the privilege of sharing in compensation is profitable. For the family immediately involved, the share of compensation is substantial, but if the other half-share has to be distributed among a large group, individual shares may be so small as not to be worth collection. The *ṣirkal* generally takes the whole of the share falling to the group, but he does not accept a corresponding obligation to contribute to compensation payments incurred by the group of which he is the representative.

Before the abolition of the shaikhdom in 1924, the corporate responsibility for paying compensation was a major factor in the organization of clans. As a large clan was able to spread the compensation so that each man had only a small contribution to make, there was a tendency for clans which were already large to increase by adoption. Tribal convention prevents a clan from refusing responsibility for any of its members or component lineages. There is nothing to prevent a lineage from changing its clan allegiance, for the sake of smaller contributions to levies for compensation and so the effect of compensation on clan membership only works in this direction. Where lineages are concerned, there is no way in which a member can be repudiated by his fellows, and a lineage member would not change his affiliation unless he had very strong reasons for doing so.

5
Family and Marriage

AFTER the group of *khowwan*, comes the family, the smallest social unit. It is headed by the eldest male, usually the father, who acts for it in the community. The average size of the family is six persons.

The family comprises a man and his wives, with any adult married sons and their wives and children, living and working together as a single economic unit. In most cases such a joint family breaks up on the death of the father, but in nine out of 30 cases in my sample of 120 families, brothers had remained together after the father's death, the eldest brother being in authority.

Each family usually occupies one island. If it owns a guest house, this is built on one side of the island, and the homestead on the other. Usually the dwelling islands are so small that they are almost completely covered by the homesteads. Children play in canoes on the water. Husband, wife and children occupy one hut. Each co-wife in a well-to-do, polygamous family should have a separate hut, and this sometimes means a separate island. A joint family which exists as a single domestic and economic unit may also be spread over several dwelling islands. Even if composed of more than one couple and their children, however, poorer families sleep together in one hut. During the day while working or resting, members of the family spend all their time together, except at meals, when the men eat first, and alone.

The scarcity of dwelling islands seems to make for closer co-operation between kinsfolk. However, the difficulty of changing residence after a quarrel does not completely prevent permanent rifts, even between members of a single family. A man, living on a small dwelling island with his brother, may not have been on speaking terms with him for years. A man can easily pretend to be preoccupied with his work, burying his head in the reeds, and so ignore the presence of anyone with whom he has broken off social relations.

Men do not normally leave their families when they marry. Only in the case of disputes between the married son or brother and the head of the family, which usually occur when the bride is not a woman of their lineage, do the newly married couple try to move away. If they are unsuccessful they will continue to live in their own hut on the family island but will be completely independent and will not be on speaking terms with the husband's family.

The father has a completely free hand in the disposal of the family property. He can beat, dismiss or divorce his wife at any time and for any reason he thinks sufficient, and has the right to keep children of either sex or any age, borne to him by a divorced or dismissed wife. He has the right to accept or reject a man asking his daughter's hand in marriage and can retain all her brideprice. As he supplies the brideprice for his son, he has the ultimate right to decide his marriage. His word is law, and every member of his family must conform to his wishes. In joint families, the father's father or the eldest brother exercises authority over every member of the joint family. He has the same rights in the joint family as the head of the elementary family has in his. Sons remain under the authority of their fathers and assist them without having the right to amass property of their own. When they marry their status changes very little. They continue to work for the family under their father's control, exercising no authority except over their own wives, and enjoying little independence.

Women have a low status in the community. They are despised by men and regarded as 'weak-minded creatures'. A woman has no right to choose her husband or to divorce him. Her status is clearly indicated by the fact that she can be given in marriage to the man who pays the highest brideprice or to the wronged party in a dispute as compensation for a crime committed by a member of her family or lineage. Mothers, especially if they are non-lineage women, have little authority over their children, though they are often loved and their wishes respected. Women are allowed no opinions in ech-Chibayish in matters concerning the management of the family finances. Ahl ech-Chibayish believe that women always give the wrong advice and, therefore, though they may be consulted, they must be contradicted. Mothers have no rights in the ultimate decisions concerning marriages in the family since these are lineage affairs and mothers might be non-lineage women. But women can accumulate small amounts of money of their own. Especially in the case of non-lineage women this may begin with the marriage payment and may be augmented by secret savings from housekeeping money, or by spinning yarn, selling eggs to the Ma'dan women traders, or selling a calf if the woman owns a cow of her own. Men do not object to their wives' accumulation of property since it can be used ultimately for the welfare of the family. The main duties of mothers are to look after their children and homes. They feed and take care of every member of the family, attend to the cattle, and do all the domestic work. They must participate in the usual family occupations, such as mat-weaving or cultivation, as fully as any other member of the family.

The behaviour of sons, naturally, changes when they attain maturity. Fathers then begin to regard them as men and some of the previous deep respect yields to familiarity and friendship. With their daughters, fathers maintain only a distant relation and when the girls attain puberty the respect for their fathers is combined with quasi-avoidance. Where questions on important matters are concerned, they use their mothers as go-betweens. The behaviour between husband and wife is based on the principle of the inferiority of the wife; though the fact that women are partners with men in the business of earning a living for the family modifies the husband's behaviour. Men in ech-Chibayish think that to accord respect or equality to wives is a kind of submission inconsistent with manhood. The wife should regard the husband as her master or lord. When talking to him, her voice should never be raised louder than his. To show their mastery over their families, husbands make a display of their superiority over their wives. The usual form of address to a wife is *wilch* or *khayba*, terms which are mainly pejorative. But husbands and wives of long standing, and especially those living alone, may in private enjoy comparative intimacy and companionship.

Economically, the family is a single unit. The family income is pooled and the head spends it on behalf of the others. No independent property is held by any member of the family, including grown-up sons. The head of the family undertakes all economic relationships outside the family. He buys its food, deals with shopkeepers and mat agents, takes and pays loans, and so on.

MARRIAGE

By Islamic law a man is allowed to take as many as four wives at a time, and among the Shi'ah sect of Islam this number can be exceeded, through the institution of *mit'a*.

The *Mit'a* (literally—'enjoyment') is a contractual marriage of limited duration. A long contract *il-'aqd il-kabir* is made to cover a much longer period than either spouse is expected to live and the marriage is considered normal in every other respect. A short contract *il-'aqd iṣ-ṣaghir* may be for a couple of days or even one night and may be entered into while a man is living temporarily far from home or while he is on pilgrimage. The long-contract *mit'a* marriage is practised among Ahl ech-Chibayish, but the second is condemned as equivalent to adultery, and no case of it was known in the village. The position, privileges and responsibilities of a long-contract *mit'a* wife do not differ from those of her four prescribed co-wives.

In ech-Chibayish polygamy is the ambition but not the achievement of most men. Among the 120 families of my census there were 118 men. 85 of them (72%) were monogamous and the rest, 33 (28%), were polygamous.

The majority of polygamous men have two wives and only a small proportion have three. The largest number of wives possessed by one man at one time was five.

Quarrels, rivalry and the fear of magic are the three distinctive features of a co-wife's life. I never met a polygamous man at ech-Chibayish who claimed a peaceful home; but owing to the strong control of the husband, he can maintain superficial cohesion and peace. On every new marriage the husband has to propitiate his previous wife or wives with clothes and money, and always has to buy the same thing for all his wives.

ELOPEMENT

Young men sometimes follow their own wishes in marriage, if they are contrary to those of their father's lineage, by elopement. Although they put their lives in danger by eloping, lovers may eventually compel their clan to accept their marriage. Elopement casts great shame on the kin of both sides, and it is held to be the duty of the woman's kin to seek and kill both the girl and her lover. Marriage by elopement is consequently rare. I recorded a case in 1953. The eloping couple usually hasten to take refuge with a headman and to obtain through the lover's kin a truce of about one month to allow the latter to settle the case by compensation. The woman's kin cannot usually object[1] to granting the truce which is negotiated through a delegation of *sāda* and *ajawid*[2] sent to them by the lover's kin. In due course another delegation goes to the woman's kin for the compensation. The woman's kin can kill the lover before he obtains a truce without being liable to pay compensation, because he is considered an adulterer: but they must pay ordinary compensation if they kill him after the truce has been granted.

The proper settlement of an elopement case is as follows: The runaway couple must marry and if the woman is already married, her husband must divorce her instantly. A marriageable girl must be given in marriage either to the eloping woman's father or kinsmen, if she was unmarried, a divorcee or a widow, or to her husband if she was married. Compensation, equivalent to the value of a second woman, which is ID 18/ooo, is paid to the eloping woman's father or kin, either in a lump sum or by instalments. A third woman, when given later in marriage at any time and for any brideprice, must forfeit the sum of ID 18/ooo from her brideprice to the eloping woman's father or kin.

The eloping woman's lineage kin do not resume ordinary relations with her even after the settlement, because elopement is one of the greatest disgraces a girl can bring upon them. If the husband is of the same lineage as his eloping wife, it is his duty to seek and kill her, as her father or brother would do, but if he is a stranger he should not intervene. He must divorce her and accept a marriageable woman as compensation.

No brideprice has to be paid by her lover for a girl who elopes with him, as this is supposed to have been included in the compensation.

INCEST

In ech-Chibayish incest prohibitions cover sexual intercourse between a

---

[1] If the kin object to granting the truce the *şirkal* has now to notify the police who take measures to prevent attempts on the lives of the girl and her lover.

[2] See below, pp. 62, 63.

man and his mother, his full and half-sisters, daughters, sister's daughters, brother's daughters, father's wives, daughters-in-law, and foster-sisters, even if they suck the mother's breast only once. The only case of incest that I heard of was that of Matūg Ahl Shfaij, who was reputed to be cohabiting with his daughter-in-law. The man was never visited or spoken to by the villagers. He was never given a cup of coffee at any guest house in the village—a great insult inferring that he was 'not like other men'. He lived in isolation, shunned by all.

BRIDEPRICE

The brideprice is paid in money, but in certain cases in cattle or furniture; clothes boxes or bedsteads especially, can be offered by the groom's family and their estimated price deducted from the brideprice, provided that the bride's parents agree. All the brideprice is normally paid in advance but an agreement can be made to leave part of it to be paid later in annual instalments, usually after the agricultural season. There is a high rate of brideprice for extra-lineage marriages, and a reduced rate for intra-lineage marriages. I have dealt with the latter in connection with lineage endogamy.

Extra-lineage brideprice ranges between ID 50/000 and ID 100/000, though in cases of widows or divorcees it may fall as low as ID 35/000. High brideprices of ID 120/000 are given for greatly desired girls, and in one case ID 180/000 was given for a girl because she was strikingly beautiful and much sought after in marriage. Conversely, undesirable men of bad reputation are asked to pay an unreasonably high brideprice, either to ward them off or to exploit them, as not many families are ready to give them brides. Hmaidi Ahl Amir, who was a dancer[1] with a very bad reputation, paid ID 100/000 for a woman who would not normally have fetched more than ID 60/000.

Though a father is entitled to seek a higher brideprice for his daughter by marrying her outside the lineage, those who exercise this right are severely criticized. The following is a good example of how fathers who desire a high brideprice must face opposition. Atshan, a man of Ahl ish-Shaikh clan, had a girl who was betrothed to the son of Mizhir, a Ṣubbi (Mandaean)[2] who had been converted to Islam. Mandaeans are considered religiously unclean by Ahl ech-Chibayish, and it is forbidden to marry with them. Mizhir offered Atshan ID 90/000, a very high brideprice, and the father readily agreed, although many blamed him for giving his daughter to a man whose father was a Mandaean. Then a man of his lineage forbade Atshan to give his daughter in this way, but he took the dispute to the ṣirkal. In the guest house, and in the presence of many tribesmen, Atshan said clearly and firmly, 'I am a needy man. I have given my daughter for ID 90/000. If my father's brother's son gives this sum, I will readily give

---

[1] Women dancers are unknown at ech-Chibayish, and dancing by boys is found only among one lineage of il-Hadadiyīn clan. It is extremely despised and considered 'shameful' and a 'gipsy occupation'.   [2] See Chapter 6.

him my daughter in marriage.' Then, after a lengthy discussion and after all the people present had expressed the opinion that it was shameful to give a girl in marriage to a Mandaean, Atshan agreed to reduce the brideprice to ID 75/000. As his lineage was not prepared to pay that amount, Atshan paid no attention to their opinions, and when they pressed the matter further, he even took the dispute to the government, at the same time going ahead with his own arrangements to give his daughter to Mizhir's son.

The father is free to keep the entire brideprice, but he is expected to supply his daughter with adequate household utensils. The usual custom is that fathers give about one-third of the brideprice to their daughters to provide themselves with clothes, bedding, a bedstead, a copper water-jug, a wash basin, a pitcher, a wooden clothes-box and a cupboard, as well as ornaments, the most essential of which is a silver anklet. Some fathers send their daughters to their grooms with only their clothes, while others put the entire brideprice at the disposal of their daughters. Fathers are expected to present some ornaments to their daughters when they become brides.

A father who has daughters, but no sons to work for him, seeks a needy young man who cannot manage to raise a brideprice and gives him one of his daughters without brideprice. The husband, called g'adi (literally, 'sitter') has to reside with his father-in-law and work for him. If at some later stage he wants to take his wife and leave her father's home, he must pay an agreed brideprice. If, on the other hand, he wants to divorce his wife, there is no question of money to be paid by either side.

Men who can afford a brideprice never agree to marry in this way, since all regard a g'adi with contempt, and in fact he is in a semi-servile relationship to his father-in-law, and exercises little authority and control over his wife.

There is another type of extra-lineage marriage in which no brideprice is paid: marriage by exchange (ṣidiq). Sisters, and more rarely daughters and brother's daughters, may be exchanged in marriage. If one of the girls is under marriageable age, that is to say, has not yet attained puberty, her kinsmen have to offer her groom a sum of money supposed to be compensation for his not yet being able to enjoy his bride fully as a wife. This type of marriage proves a failure in many cases, simply because the kin of each girl have to send back their daughter-in-law if their own daughter has been dismissed or divorced by her husband, regardless of whether or not she and her husband love each other.

After the death of the wife, the husband may marry her sister. There is no obligation or right on the part of the husband to claim his deceased wife's sister, but if the deceased wife has left small children, it is thought that their mother's sister would look after them better than a stranger stepmother would do. Similarly there is no obligation for levirate marriage, but many men marry their brother's widows if the brothers have left children for whose unbringing they are responsible. Some, however, think that it is 'disgusting to tread one's own brother's bed', i.e. to cohabit with a brother's widow. Marriage with the father's widow is forbidden by religion, as such a woman is regarded as a mother. Marriages with father's brother's or mother's brother's widows are greatly despised, but some such cases are known to have taken place in the village.

DIVORCE

The main grounds for divorce in ech-Chibayish are adultery or barrenness. Adultery by women is punishable by death at the hands of her kin or by divorce from her husband. If his wife is not of his lineage, a husband is expected to send her home, divorce her and leave her punishment to her kin. The adulteress's kin usually kill her secretly. Adultery of her husband, on the other hand, cannot be grounds for divorce for the wife. If a bride is found not to be a virgin this can be grounds for divorce.

There are various other minor reasons for divorce, such as the bad behaviour of the wife, her misappropriation of, or extravagance with, the household money, and sometimes the influence or conspiracies of co-wives.

Husbands can, at any time and for any reason, divorce their wives. If the husband has a recognized reason or if the wife wishes to leave her husband, he has the right to the return of the brideprice he gave, together with all the expenses of the marriage ceremonies; but if he has no good grounds for divorce he has claim to neither. In certain cases both sides wish to dissolve the marriage and agree that a certain sum, usually the brideprice only, is to be paid back to the husband, either when his divorced wife remarries or within a certain period. This type of divorce is considered irreligious.

Divorcees usually return to live among their own kin and are not asked in marriage. Ahl ech-Chibayish prefer widows to divorcees as there is always a presupposition of the latter's bad conduct. A divorcee who re-marries is usually worth about half the usual brideprice.

A widow is much respected and helped both by her own kin and that of her husband. If she has children she has a chance of being remarried in her deceased husband's lineage. Otherwise, she may either remain in her husband's home or live near a brother-in-law. Childless widows often return to their kin and have greater chances of remarriage. The husband's kin are responsible for offering the widow any help she needs until she remarries. If a widow who has children wishes to live with her own kin, her husband's lineage do not object. She is supposed to leave her children with their lineage, but the deceased husband's kin usually agree to leave the children with her.

6

The Traditional System of Social Stratification

IN ech-Chibayish five social classes are traditionally recognized. First are the 'holy men', second the ex-ruling clan, third the heads of commoner clans and lineages together with other commoners, fourth the slaves and last the foreign Subba.

THE 'HOLY MEN'

Is-sāda claim descent from Muhammad the Prophet. All are supposed to be descendants of one or another of the Imams through Fatima, the Prophet's daughter, and her husband, Ali Ibn Abu Talib, the Prophet's cousin, and thus hold a highly esteemed religious position. There is no way of ascertaining whether a man is really a direct descendant of the Prophet, since there are no authentic records and the whole matter depends entirely on claim. Many people in the marsh region and other communities pretend to be *sāda*, since such a claim confers a high social prestige, with possibilities of material gain. The only precaution taken is that the claimant sometimes changes his place of residence, so that his claim may not be examined too thoroughly.

Because these reputed 'holy men' enjoy high prestige among the Shi'ah Marsh Dwellers, many of them have come to the marsh region. They live, in general, by begging, and on whatever concession of land and crops the shaikhs may grant them. They exploit the ignorant Marsh Dwellers by claiming supernatural powers to cure maladies or cause misfortunes; and they make a great deal of money by practising magic rites.

At ech-Chibayish there are eight families of 'holy men' comprising altogether about 50 individuals. Six of these families are known to have been living in the village for many generations. The *sāda* of ech-Chibayish differ in many respects from the 'holy men' of the other marsh communities. None of them is known to have practised any magic or claimed supernatural power. This is probably connected with the unusual care and generosity shown to them by the shaikhs and with their consequent economic security. Apart from their claimed descent and (in the case of one or two) the wearing of blue head-cloths,[1] the *sāda* of ech-Chibayish are quite

[1] The *sāda* of Iraq distinguish themselves by wearing either black, blue or green turbans, or blue head cloths according to the *imam* from whom they claim descent.

ordinary individuals in their way of life. Only two earn their living by begging. The others are traders, cultivators or mat-weavers. Two of the *sāda* families, those of Bait Sayid Khalaf, are by far the richest people in the village. They are the main grain and mat-traders and are also the main moneylenders of ech-Chibayish. Two other *sāda* families, Bait Sayid Baqir is-Sayid Ali and Bait Sayid Yousif is-Sayid Jabir, are mat-traders and shopkeepers, who come twelfth and thirteenth among the 20 rich men of the village.[1] Two of the remaining four *sāda* families live by cultivation and mat-weaving and the other two by hiring their labour or by occasional cultivation.

Like all the Shi'ah of Iraq, the inhabitants of ech-Chibayish look upon *is-sāda* as sacred people, 'the sons of the Messenger of God' (*awlad rasūl allah*), so that respect and veneration are paid to them as a religious duty. Ahl ech-Chibayish take oaths by *is-sāda*, especially by one or two of them known to be scrupulous in their religion. In matters such as betrothal, paying compensation for a crime, sending a delegation to soften the feelings of an injured man, it is preferably a *sayyid* who leads the delegation, because he is never refused if he makes a demand or request. *Is-sāda* sit at the best places in the guest houses and are given priority wherever they go. The clan heads do not take their share of the crop from *is-sāda* who cultivate their lands.

Being descendants of the Prophet, *is-sāda* are supposed to be very scrupulous in religious matters and far removed from the struggle for gain, more especially if this struggle involves usury, which is strongly condemned by Islam. In practice, four of the eight families of *is-sāda* at ech-Chibayish almost monopolize the business of moneylending. The other two *sāda* families do the same in connection with the mat trade. In fact, these four *sāda* families not only depart from the religious duties imposed on them as Moslems and their status as 'Sons of Muhammad', but they seem to be using their religious status for material gain. People believe in them and never think of suing them in cases of dispute. At the mere mention of the oath, 'By my grandfather, the Messenger of God', a tribesman has to believe what the *sayyid* claims, or otherwise he becomes an infidel. This oath, however, has always been used as a means of gain and cheating. But Ahl ech-Chibayish are quite aware of the *sāda* traders' attitude in business and, consequently, do not look upon them with the same respect as they do the non-business *sāda* who do not allow the lust for gain to get the better of them.

It should be stressed that *is-sāda* is not a caste, or a clan. This applies to every part of Iraq. The *sāda* of ech-Chibayish live scattered over the village; five families live with Ahl ish-Shaikh clan, two with Ahl Ghrīj, and one with Ahl Limabir. The eight families are attached to the clans with whom they live. There is no agnatic relationship among the *sāda* families, not even between *sāda* of the same clan. Nevertheless, the *sāda*

[1] For details, see Chapter 11.

tend to marry among themselves. There is no strict endogamy as a few cases of inter-marriage with non-*sāda* families have been recorded in the village; but they are rare.

Il-muwamna are the religious agents of *il-mujtahid*, the chief religious head of the Shi'ah sect at the holy city of in-Najaf. Such an agent, referred to locally as *mūman*, and addressed as *shaikh*, is *mukhawal shar'i*, religiously authorized to settle matters covered by Islamic law, such as marriage, divorce and inheritance. *Il-mūman* is supposed to be a graduate of one of the religious schools of in-Najaf and lives on what money people give him for his religious services. In addition, he has other important functions. He conducts the *qrāyat* mourning ceremonies performed throughout the first ten days of *Muḥarram* (an Arabic month) to commemorate the death of the Imam Husain and his kin and followers in the Battle of Karbala. *Il-muwamna* are paid for conducting such ceremonies from the communal contributions paid by the mourners, who do their utmost to pay as much as they can because they believe that the more they pay, the greater the religious reward.

At ech-Chibayish there is one *mūman* who is a graduate of a religious school and thus fully authorized in all religious matters. He is not a native of ech-Chibayish but is responsible as far as religious matters are concerned for ech-Chibayish and il-Midina, a village about ten miles down the river, and divides his time between the two. There is also a family whose late head was an authorized *mūman*. After his death, two of his sons, though uneducated in religious affairs, began to perform some simple religious practices, such as reading prayers or conducting *qrāyat* ceremonies, but neither enjoys the same prestige as the authorized *mūman*. During the month of *Muḥarram*, one or two of the numerous touring *muwamna* come to the village to conduct the *qrāyat* ceremonies of which there are about 15.

Il-muwamna, especially graduates of religious schools, are highly respected and classed with the *sāda*. They are usually entirely devoted to their religious duties and do not take up any secular business. But some of them, especially those who are unauthorized, practise begging, and exploit the ignorant Marsh Dwellers, particularly those of Amara region. The *mūman* of ech-Chibayish, Shaikh Mhammad Ali Hmūzi, was devoted to his duties; he enjoyed high prestige in the village because of his religious knowledge and because he did not beg.

THE EX-RULING CLAN

Ahl Khayūn are the noble clan of Beni Isad. They trace their descent to one Dahla 13 generations back from the eldest living members of the clan.

For four centuries Ahl Khayūn were the rulers of Beni Isad. Till the abolition of the shaikhdom in 1924, they lived as a military aristocracy. They exercised great power and treated all other members of the tribe as subjects, or serfs. A tribesman was always supposed to be at the disposal of the noble clan for any services that might be required of him. The shaikhs, the heads of Ahl Khayūn, used fines and imprisonment in their mud fortresses as the usual method of punishment. The shaikh and his kinsmen appropriated most of the produce of the land and collected dues on date palms and cattle. The shaikh used to share with the fathers even the brideprices of girls. The Khayūni used to have the undisputed right to insult, beat or maltreat any tribesman. Any member of the clan had the right to intervene in any dispute. In travelling, or any kind of labour, the Khayūni could order any number of Beni Isad to offer their services. If he needed money he would collect from the tribe, because a Khayūni was not expected to work; his only task was to rule.

When the Shaikhdom was abolished, and the government established a strong administrative unit in the village,[1] Ahl Khayūn found themselves in a changed situation. They would not submit to the government and some of them took to leading groups of outlaws and thieves to the Hor. They caused much trouble before they were finally defeated and banished. Others left for Amara and other districts hoping for a change of conditions but returned later to ech-Chibayish. One or two of the wiser and more peace-loving men, such as Abdil-Hadi Ahl Khayūn, remained in the village, and even helped and supported the government in its efforts to maintain law and order. Later the government allotted salaries and rich lands outside ech-Chibayish to some of them.

To-day the great bulk of Ahl Khayūn, about 30 men, live at ech-Chibayish, but there are branches of the clan at Gurmat Ali and Amara, and the last shaikh divides his time between Baghdad, where he maintains a modern house, and his lands about 50 miles away in the Diyala Province. At ech-Chibayish, two families of Ahl Khayūn live on salaries received from the government as 'banishment stipend', one lives on the salary of its head who is a government employee in the village, one lives on previous savings, whilst the remaining ten families live by land holding, trade and cultivation.

Ahl Khayūn are now in a state of transition from their previous high status to that of ordinary citizens. Some of them have begun, for the first time in the history of Ahl Khayūn, to cultivate land and tend cattle. Others have entered government service as clerks and soldiers, and some have taken up jobs which even the ordinary member of Beni Isad despise, such as running a motor launch service.

Except for a certain superficial respect, which is indeed only accorded to those who are really 'good fellows', Beni Isad do not to-day allow Ahl Khayūn any of their previous privileges.

Ahl Khayūn, however, still maintain in general a higher standard of living. Except for one or two families, they live in better huts equipped with good furniture, such as chairs, wardrobes, boxes for keeping clothes, etc. They wear clothes of the same style as those of the natives but always

[1] See Chapter 3.

more luxurious. Their women dress far better than the other women, using jewellery and cosmetics. They eat food which is nearer to that of the townspeople and better and richer than that of the rest of Ahl ech-Chibayish. In their homes they maintain certain traditions about which they are very particular. For example, the younger members of the clan, though younger only by a single day, must show respect by kissing the hand of the elder and rising in his presence in any public place. Women are permitted neither to eat with nor in the presence of men, and may not go to bed before them. No Khayūni should paddle or pole himself in a canoe. The majority of Ahl Khayūn are literate.

The strongest Ahl Khayūn tradition is that of clan endogamy which is strict in the case of their womenfolk and only occasionally broken in the case of their men. Since the days of Shaikh Hasan Ahl Khayūn, not a single Khayūniya woman has been given in marriage outside the clan. But Ahl Khayūn men do sometimes marry outside the clan. Nearly all Ahl Khayūn shaikhs were married to one or more non-Khayūnia women in addition to their Khayūniya wives. Although few men among the present younger generations of Ahl Khayūn are married to outsider wives as well, this tendency to out-marriage has given rise to a surplus of unmarried women in the clan. In 1953 there were six very old unmarried women of Ahl Khayūn and there were a number who were passing the marriageable age. Understandably Ahl Khayūn women resist strongly any attempt on the part of the men to marry wives from other clans.

HEADS OF COMMONER CLANS AND LINEAGES: THE AJAWĪD

The shaikhs of Beni Isad used to choose distinguished men, one from each clan, and appoint them as their agents in those clans. When the last Shaikh was overthrown, the government wisely appointed all those who were agents at that time as *şirkals*, each in his own clan. Also, the government ratified the lineage headmen in their positions and made them *mukhtārs*.

Each clan contains a number of men who are members of large lineages and known to be 'good fellows', helpful and peace-loving, with a good knowledge of tribal law and traditions and sound, trustworthy opinions. Such men are known as *ajawīd it-tayfa*. Together with the *şirkals* and *mukhtārs*, they constitute a subdivision of the third class of the ech-Chibayish community. They do not differ from the other commoners either in traditions or customs, nor do they intermarry to any extent. Except for the *şirkals*, who are relatively wealthy as a result of land holding and other dues, and who with the *mukhtārs* enjoy some political power, they differ little economically from the other commoners. Their rights and privileges derive from the respect they enjoy in the community and from the influence they exert.

OTHER COMMONERS

The commoners are the vast majority of Ahl ech-Chibayish. They live by mat-weaving, cultivation and seasonal labour migration. They keep cattle and most families have date palms on their dwelling islands. In general they are poor and the majority are heavily in debt either to mat traders or moneylenders.

It has already been mentioned that in the past the commoners suffered a great deal from exploitation by their shaikhs. But nowadays this is not possible. The government is there to check any abuse of power on the part of ṣirkals. The commoners have full freedom to follow any occupation, to cultivate anywhere they like and live in any part of the village. They can even change their lineage or clan by process of adoption. In their personal affairs, such as marriage, divorce, mortgage, sale and other similar matters, the commoners are quite free and the ṣirkals or the mukhtārs cannot legally intervene.

The commoners form one class equal in rights and obligations, but certain distinctions affect an individual's personal prestige. Thus it is more distinguished to belong to certain clans, or to follow certain occupations than others. A member of Ahl Ghrīj or Ahl Khatir clan is, for example, less respected in the community than a member of Ahl ish-Shaikh or Ahl Anaisi clan. According to tradition, some occupations count as beneath the dignity of a Beni Isad.

SLAVES (IL-'ABĪD)[1]

During the old days of the shaikhdom a distinctive feature of the shaikh's household was the large number of slaves employed as household servants, coffee men, paddlers, messengers and agents. All these were African negroes imported from Arabia and sold in the slave markets of Basra and Baghdad during the old days of the slave trade. Though slaves were then treated as chattels, they were, at ech-Chibayish, monopolized by the shaikhs and Ahl Khayūn. Any slave outside Khayūni households had originally come from them.

In those days, when even the free tribesmen were serfs to their shaikhs, the slaves were without legal or social status. At ech-Chibayish they used to live in their masters' households 'for the food of their bellies' and what clothes their masters cared to allow them. Their masters controlled their marriages. They could not own or inherit property. If a slave was involved in a criminal case, his master settled the case and paid or received his compensation. Their masters beat them, fettered them, and if any suspicions were aroused of sexual relations between them and their masters' womenfolk, they were killed.

The slave's main duties were either inside the shaikh's household, preparing and serving coffee at the guesthouse, bringing fodder for the cattle, paddling the shaikh's canoe and so on, or outside the household. Those

[1] 'Abid in colloquial Arabic means 'slaves', and indicates 'lack of freedom', 'inferiority in status', but does not indicate 'chattel'. If the latter meaning is to be implied the word 'abid should be followed by the word mamlūk, which means 'owned'.

employed outside acted as liaison officers between the shaikh and tribesmen, and were chosen from among the more faithful and intelligent. They
were employed as messengers, to pass on the shaikh's orders, or as agents
in the fields, to supervise cultivation and crop division. Those appointed
to represent the shaikh in his widely-scattered estates attained high
authority and accumulated fortunes of their own. A few slaves enjoyed
the full confidence of their masters, and consequently were second in
command to them. Some even built guest houses, which were frequented
by people seeking their favour. The personal servant of Shaikh Salim Ahl
Khayūn, for example, used to dress like the shaikh himself and bathe in
perfumed water, and paid a large sum of money as a brideprice for a
'white' wife whom he brought from Baghdad.

When the shaikhdom was abolished, the slaves were suddenly left without masters. The shaikh was arrested, the majority of Ahl Khayūn were
living as outlaws in the Hor, and the few Khayūni families who remained
at ech-Chibayish were too poor even to maintain themselves. At that time
there were at least 50 slave families. Some of them migrated to Basra and
Baghdad to work and live as labourers or to join the newly-formed army
and police forces. Most of those who stayed in the village left their masters'
households and began to earn a living as free men.

To-day there are only 22 families of slave origin (109 individuals) in
ech-Chibayish. All of them have Negroid features. Only six of these
families are still living as slaves in the old sense of the word: five families
working in four Khayūni households, and one family in the household of
a lineage headman of Ahl Ghrīj clan. Every one of these six families had
been compelled for various reasons to remain in their previous status. Two
of those who remained in the village agreed to return to two Khayūni
families as servants but not as slaves; they were paid monthly salaries and
each maintained their own hut and household. Eight of the remaining 14
families of slaves are earning their living by cultivation and mat-weaving,
and six by living on salaries received from 12 of their members employed
as soldiers and government employees.

The slaves, like their previous masters, have adjusted themselves to
living as ordinary tribesmen. They speak of themselves now as 'Beni Isad'
and not 'abīd Ahl Khayūn'. The relation between them and Ahl Khayūn
is that of fellow tribesmen, except in the case of those who are still living
in their master's households. They earn their living freely and enjoy full
rights in the community. In many tribal affairs, such as mourning ceremonies and compensation, they are treated as ordinary tribesmen, and
have no extra obligations in the community.

Though the six slave families living in their masters' households continue to live as their fathers did before them, they can enjoy full freedom
if they wish. No master can now stop a slave from leaving him, and there
is none of the former cruelty shown to the slave, because he can run away
if maltreated. Besides, owing to the full legal status now enjoyed by a slave,

legal action can be taken against the master. In fact, these six slave families do enjoy considerable freedom in their personal affairs. The link between them and their masters is not of the old bondage of slavery but of loyalty to the families in whose service they have been living for so long. Moreover, such a life ensures the slaves an easy security. The masters need their service and keep them because it is not possible to find servants at ech-Chibayish. The real situation of these ex-slaves and their masters is quasi-slavery or voluntarily suspended freedom.

But there is no intermarriage between ex-slaves and the rest of Ahl ech-Chibayish. There have been rare cases when masters fell in love with their female slaves and married them; but the offspring, called 'half-breed', though free, cannot get 'white' wives; and they usually marry either slaves or half-breeds like themselves. It has not been known in the village for a freewoman to be given in marriage to a slave. The case of Shaikh Salim's personal servant, referred to previously, was the only case in which a slave was married to a freewoman and, as has been stated, she was a towns-woman from Baghdad. In a case of elopement which concerned il-Hadadi-yīn and Ahl Wnais clans many years ago, the eloping girl's kin demanded exceptionally high compensation because the lover had some slave traits in his features and it was therefore believed that his mother had borne him illegitimately through liaison with a slave. It was a double disgrace that a man suspected of being a half-breed should have eloped with their free-born daughter.

IS-ṢUBBA (THE MANDAEANS)[1]

The Ṣubba are a religious minority living in southern Iraq, mainly near the marshes and on the river banks because water is so important to them for ceremonial ablutions. They claim to be followers of St. John the Baptist, and have certain holy books written by hand in a language akin to Syriac and Aramaic, called Mandaean. Their chief rite is ceremonial ablution. Water, they hold, is the element which gives life to body and soul; they practise ablution as often as they can, and everything eaten must be washed in running water. Their priests slaughter the animals which they eat and perform marriage and funeral ceremonies. They have certain feasts and days of fasting. They never intermarry with non-Ṣubba and avoid close contact with those of different faith. They number about 4,000 souls in Iraq and are mainly occupied as blacksmiths, silversmiths and canoe- and boat-builders.

The two main centres of Ṣubba in Iraq are Amara and Sūg ish-Shyūkh regions. Until 40 years ago about 170 Ṣubba families used to live at ech-Chibayish, but all migrated gradually to il-Gurna and Sūg ish-Shyūkh, because during the period of political instability from 1914 to 1924 they were frequently violated and plundered by Ahl Khayūn. All the boats and

---

[1] On the Mandaeans, see the works of E. S. Drower (E. S. Stevens), particularly *The Mandaeans of Iraq and Iran*, Oxford, 1957.

the canoes used by Ahl ech-Chibayish used to be locally built by Ṣubba, but owing to their growing outside contacts, Ahl ech-Chibayish have now begun to buy their canoes and boats from li-Hwair, a marshy village about 15 miles down the river.

There are now only three Ṣubba families living at ech-Chibayish and these consist of only 13 individuals. All three families are blacksmiths and manufacture fishing-spears, sickles, reed-splitters, spades, nails and so on. They never practise cultivation or mat-weaving, but they keep cattle.

Being non-Moslems, the Ṣubba are considered religiously polluted. The people of ech-Chibayish do not eat with them nor drink from receptacles they have used. No question of intermarriage ever arises. The one known exception at ech-Chibayish was an elopement between a slave and a Ṣubbiya girl. In this case the girl's kin made great efforts to arrest the eloping couple and subsequently refused to accept compensation according to the tribal law because they did not want to give their daughter in marriage, as the law required, to a man who was a Moslem and a slave as well.

As a result of the constant plunder and injuries they suffered in the past, the three families who chose to remain at ech-Chibayish obtained adoption into Ahl Awaiti lineage of Ahl ish-Shaikh clan, who were then notorious plunderers and thieves, so that they might enjoy greater security. In spite of this adoption and residence, and though they share the compensations with all other members of the tribe, the Subba, nevertheless, neither settle their cases through the ṣirkal of the clan into which they are adopted, nor participate in any of the tribe's activities. For protection and justice they depend entirely on the government.

As I have tried to show, social stratification among the Beni Isad is entirely determined by birth in the case of the five traditional classes, is-sāda, Ahl Khayūn, the commoners, il-'abīd and the Subba. In the case of the two subdivisions of the commoner class, however, the determinants are not inherited but acquired—wealth, good conduct, knowledge of tribal traditions and law. A commoner can become a member of the ajawīd, a head of his lineage, or a ṣirkal, and conversely one of the ajawīd may lose his prestige and be counted as an ordinary commoner, and a ṣirkal or mukhtār can be dismissed from his position. In the case of the appointment of ṣirkals, however, heredity is taken into consideration. Mobility is possible only between these two subdivisions.

The class structure cuts across the lineage and clan system in the case of the classes of 'holy men', commoners and slaves, since members of these classes can exist in any lineage or clan. But Ahl Khayūn form a distinct clan, and the Ṣubba, though adopted into Ahl ish-Shaikh clan, are in fact not counted as clansmen.

Barriers between social classes were more rigid before the abolition of the shaikhdom than they are now. Both Ahl Khayūn and the slaves now

A. Four elders

B. Lughmaija channel

2

A. A hut built on a reed platform

B. A hut during the flood

A. A canoe shop

B. A floating platform poled by two men

4

A. A floating platform with hut and buffaloes

B. A youth milking a buffalo

A. A guest house

B. A reed hut in an early stage of building

A. A man and boy cutting reed

B. A family splitting and skinning reed.

A. Mats stored ready for collection

B. Fishermen's nets spread to dry in the sun

A. A dwelling island

B. A large sailing boat with labour immigrants to Basra

mix with the rest of the tribe—Ahl Khayūn losing most of their old privileges and rights, and the slaves gaining new ones. After 30 years of such drastic political, economic and social change, Ahl Khayūn are a distinct social class only by virtue of their history and birth, and this is also the case with the slaves. Though the hereditary barrier is still in operation for the 'holy men', the fact that all of them began to earn their living in various ways immediately after the abolition of the shaikhdom, has destroyed a great deal of the old character of this class. Four families of 'holy men' practise usury; two individuals even beg for their living; none of the sayids at ech-Chibayish live nowadays on a generous income accruing to them directly from their hereditary religious status, as they used to before the abolition of the shaikhdom. No-one is there to-day to give them 'the fifth of their grandfather'.[1]

Contact among the various classes is quite free and not restricted by any rules or traditions, except in connection with the Ṣubba where it does not go beyond talking and touching. The 'holy-men', Ahl Khayūn, the ṣirkals and other commoners, and former slaves, sit down together, deal and talk freely with one another. The rule of endogamy is strict only where the Ṣubba are concerned, though normally Beni Isad do not intermarry with former slaves. This is mainly because of an ideal of racial purity, the slaves being of Negro descent. Ahl Khayūn also practise a restricted form of clan endogamy, but only where their women are concerned, and it is doubtful whether now, owing to the surplus of unmarried women in the clan and to the gradual weakening of Ahl Khayūn's traditions, this custom will be long preserved.

Occupational distinctions are used by Beni Isad to distinguish themselves from outsiders (as will be seen in chapter 12) but they are now less important than formerly for the differentiation of status within the tribe; nor is there now a clear correlation between social status and economic advantage. For example, among the 'holy men', the highest social class, there are land holders, shopkeepers, employees, cultivators and beggars. Similarly, slaves are shopkeepers, cultivators and mat-weavers, and this is the case with the other classes. No man is banned from any occupation by reason of his social class; and wealth and poverty in themselves do not determine social standing.

[1] According to the Shi'ah doctrine, is-sāda have a claim of one-fifth of all the property of Shi'ah Moslems. At ech-Chibayish the shaikhs used to get this from the tribesmen and paid it to is-sāda, but now none of Ahl ech-Chibayish pay this fifth except when a tribesman wants to go on a pilgrimage to Mecca, when it is believed to be a necessary pre-requisite. Even in this case the fifth is paid for the cash property only and at in-Najaf, the religious centre of the Shi'ah, where it is distributed according to a certain system among all the sāda of the country or used for other religious purposes.

F

7

The Guest House *(il-muḍīf)*

Il-muḍīf, literally 'the place of hospitality', is an old feature of bedouin social life. In the pre-Islamic era the shaikhs of the bedouin tribes of Arabia used to keep 'guest house' tents to feed and accommodate travellers in the desert or as meeting places for all the men of the tribe. As hospitality was a major duty for all bedouins, guest houses were an essential adjunct to their life, and much of the prestige of the shaikhs of those days was based on the hospitality they showed to their guests.

Guest houses are found throughout the marsh region, but they are less common in the eastern group of Marsh Dwellers than in the western, where the tribes still maintain many bedouin customs. While the old bedouin guest house used to be mainly a place of hospitality and occasionally a war council chamber, in the marsh region it is a social club in which tribesmen gather every day to hold their courts of justice and ceremonies, and where hospitality to strangers is only occasionally offered.

Under Ahl Khayūn leadership, building and maintaining guest houses among the Beni Isad was the sole prerogative of the shaikhs and other leading members of the Ahl Khayūn clan. But when the shaikhdom began to wane and was later abolished, many tribesmen, especially the newly created *ṣirkals* and *mukhtārs*, began to build their own.

In 1953 there were about 600 guest houses in ech-Chabayish to 1,604 families: the ownership of a guest house has become a symbol of prestige for ordinary tribesmen, whereas it used to be the sole privilege of the shaikh.

The guest house is a huge hut built of bundles of stout reeds and reed mats. The bundles, made of reeds tied with ropes of plaited and twisted reeds, are set at regular intervals in two rows, and the heads of each facing pair are bent over and interwoven carefully to form a perfect arch. Thin transverse bundles are bound to the arches, covering the whole structure and ending at a height of about three feet from the ground on each side. A latticework of reeds is then inserted and tied to cover the opening between the lowest transverse bundle and the ground, to admit air and keep the building cool in summer. Finally, the whole framework is covered by large overlapping reed mats. The two end walls are constructed of strong palm trunks covered with reeds and strengthened by vertical bundles with matting and latticework. At each end wall there is a small doorless entrance in the middle and two other smaller openings at its side.

Such guest houses, towering over the smaller dwelling huts of the village, vary from 24 to 98 feet in length and from 10 to 15 feet in width. The number of arches ranges from 7 to 17. Traditionally they should be an odd number.

Clan guest houses are usually bigger than the others and act as political and social centres. Coffee is served in them every morning. At sunrise, coffee is ready and tribesmen begin to arrive to spend an hour or two before beginning their daily work. The clan head should attend the morning session every day, and if he is prevented by sickness or other reasons from attending, the guest house must be kept open and coffee served, a brother or a son deputizing for him. Anyone, clansmen or non-clansmen, even strangers, can attend and drink coffee.

In the guest houses of the lineages, coffee is served occasionally in the afternoon and for feasts and religious ceremonies. Some lineage headmen and notables have a fixed day on the afternoon of which they make coffee. Others make it only on certain occasions, when they are visited by a stranger, when they have received urgent news which they are anxious to impart, or when there are important matters to discuss with lineage members or neighbours. In such cases the pounding of the coffee beans in the big brass mortar serves as a bell to summon all tribesmen within sound, and the villagers are experienced in locating accurately the distant sound of a mortar. Less coffee is prepared for afternoon sessions, as a smaller number of men attend. Only members of the lineage and neighbours usually come, but friends or near clansmen who catch the sound of the mortar, hear the men chatting, or see the smoke, may join the rest.

Large guest houses are usually rebuilt about every 15 years and must be repaired twice in the second half of this period. Smaller ones may stand longer, unless there is a succession of high floods.

Clan guest houses are built by all adult males in the clan, and the clan head decides the date on which building should begin. If all adult males cannot attend and contribute to certain stages of the building, such as the day of pitching the arch bundles or the day of binding and tying them at least one member from each family should contribute on its behalf. On occasions when fewer men are needed, the clan head asks for labour only from those who live nearest to him, from his particular friends, or from men who have fewer economic responsibilities. The enormous amount of reeds needed for the huge arches and long transverse bundles have to be cut and brought from distant places in the marsh. The extra-large mats are specially woven and offered by each of the families of the clan.

Lineages tend to act as separate units in building the clan guest house. Each takes the responsibility of pitching, bending and covering with fine skinned reeds one arch which may ultimately be known by its name. Different lineages compete among themselves to produce the best work possible and one or two lineages may even challenge others, offer a prize and appoint judges of the contest. While working, each lineage chants war songs and sometimes songs may be especially composed to praise the owner. Men of high social standing—*sāda* or distinguished members of Ahl Khayūn clan—may come to honour the owner and to encourage the tribesmen to do their utmost. Their role in the construction of the guest house is an honorary one. They watch, give directions and undertake certain symbolic tasks, such as helping to pitch the arches.

The owner of the guest house has to offer all the labourers two meals on every day of work. When the guest house of Ahl ish-Shaikh clan was built in February-March 1953, the work was spread over 28 days. On the two big days of pitching and bending the arches, about 150 men took part for six to eight hours daily.

Though all the local raw materials are provided by the clan, and all labour, except that of the artisan who supervises the building, is offered free by members of the clan, nevertheless building a clan guest house is very expensive. The guest house of Ahl ish-Shaikh clan cost ID 140/250. ID 99/150 was spent on food for the labourers, and ID 41/100 on cordage, date-palm trunks, wages for the artisan and for Ma'dan labourers to bring in earth, etc. This money is provided by the clan head from his own pocket.

Building the guest house of a lineage headman or a notable is the responsibility of his lineage, but friends and neighbours may help, especially on the two big occasions of the building. These small guest houses cost between ID 50/000 and ID 100/000

Whatever other qualifications a tribesman may possess, he may yet fail to be recognized as a 'good fellow' if he does not maintain a guest house; and there were cases in ech-Chibayish of people who lost their prestige because they had neglected hospitality for material gain.

All the chiefs of the clans and the lineage headmen own guest houses, as it is a pre-requisite of their status. For any ordinary tribesman who wishes to own one, adequate funds are not in themselves enough. The most important item in the construction is the communal labour which cannot be secured unless he has already attained a degree of prestige among his lineage and clan. The size of the guest house is controlled by the social status of its owner. The higher his social rank, the larger he may build it. The largest guest house in ech-Chibayish used to be that of Shaikh Salim Ahl Khayūn, which was erected on Ahl Khayūn's traditional number of 13 arches. When he rebuilt it on 15 arches, he was criticized; and when he was overthrown and his new guest house was burnt during the disciplinary action taken against him by the government, many believed that his misfortunes were caused by his overlooking tribal traditions, including the number of arches of his guest house. In 1947, his son, Thaban Ahl Khayūn, who was neither a shaikh nor a *ṣirkal*, built a guest house even larger than that of his father, on 17 arches, and was severely and openly criticized.

In view of the low standard of living of the majority of the people, and the high cost of building, the possession of a large guest house is a solid indication of the material wealth of its owner.

Tribesmen used to gather in the guest houses of their shaikhs and leaders, to listen to their decisions concerning warfare, disputes and economic activities. The ownership of a guest house gives prestige because the tribesmen gather round the owner to 'drink his coffee and listen to his words'. A man who has been disgraced by the adultery or elopement of one of his womenfolk should 'turn down his coffee pots' and close his guest house until he avenges his honour either by killing the culprit or by getting compensation. Unless he can do so, no-one would consider him fit to be visited, or his coffee to be drunk. Similarly a son cannot build a guest house while his father is alive, as a son must not try to acquire greater prestige than his father.

Since the First World War, contact with the outside world and the impact of new economic and administrative changes has created a new class of traders, shopkeepers and employees in ech-Chibayish, the very nature of whose business conflicts with tribal conventions. Most members of this new class have had to abandon their fathers' guest houses or the guest houses they maintained before they became involved in business. They found they could no longer afford the time to act as host in the long coffee-drinking sessions, they felt less interest in the long discussion of tribal affairs and they grudged the expense. However, those who sacrificed this most valued feature of tribal life for material gain lost immeasurable prestige in the eyes of their tribesmen. Some members of this new class tried to compensate by allocating a room in their brick-built houses as guest room where on feasts and other occasions guests are received and tea or even coffee is served. Still the people do not consider that brick guest rooms compare with the reed guest house. While his father's guest house was being built, Tariq Ahl Khayūn told me that they could have built a brick guest room at less cost than that of a reed guest house, but the clansmen wanted a reed guest house in which to forgather. A notable of Ahl ish-Shaikh, a well-to-do shop owner who lived in a brick-built house, declared that he was determined to build himself a reed guest house because his brick guest room did not compensate for the lack of its reed prototype. He added: 'The right place for coffee pots is in the reed *mudif* and not in the brick guest room.'

The emergence of this new commercial class and the presence in the village of a number of policemen, teachers and officials, who cannot all attend guest houses because of their work, has given rise to commercially run cafés. In 1953 there were four of these cafés where tea (not coffee) could be bought and where people came at any time in the day or evening to spend their leisure. Market prices and commodities and gossip about the village administrative headquarters are the main topics of conversation in these cafés; and gambling, abhorrent to Ahl ech-Chibayish, takes place, especially late at night. There is no room for any of the traditions or etiquette of the old guest houses, and people of social standing in the tribe never go to these cafés.

THE FUNCTION OF THE GUEST HOUSE IN THE COMMUNITY

The guest house is of considerable importance in the community as a social centre, a political conference chamber and a court of justice. Tribesmen gather there to spend their leisure in drinking coffee, smoking and exchanging news. In the guest house they hold their marriage ceremonies, their funeral ceremonies, and the ritual ceremonies to commemorate the murder of the Imam Husain in the Battle of Karbala. Each clan guest house holds ten-day ceremonies on behalf of all the clansmen, and some other notables of the village also hold special ceremonies in their own guest houses. At the two feasts 'Īd Ramdhān and 'Īd dhiyya, every owner of a guest house must prepare sufficient quantities of coffee, tea, orange or lemon sherbet and cigarettes to entertain all those who come to offer their greetings. Any traveller or stranger should be entertained with coffee and food and accommodated in the guest house as long as he wishes to stay.

The clan guest houses have a further function in the community. They are conference chambers where all political concerns of the clan, such as taxation, land problems and the relations with the government are discussed. Previously the war council (*amra*) used to be held in them, and nowadays councils of *ajawīd it-tayfa*. The most accurate way of testing public opinion is to throw the problem to the tribesmen assembled in your guest house and listen to their comments and reactions.

Complaints are lodged and cases settled in the clan guest houses. If the case has to go to the government, all contact between the *ṣirkal* and the two contesting parties takes place in the building and compensation rates are fixed and paid there.

The guest house is a sacred place; people take oaths in the guest house of their clan, or in that of a *sayyid* or a Khayūni chief. Those who have a dear desire sometimes make a wish in a guest house. Standing bare-headed and touching one of its pillars they solemnly utter the wish, exactly as they might do in the tomb of an Imam. An offender or culprit can take sanctuary in a guest house, even in that of his enemy. During the last days of Shaikh Hasan Ahl Khayūn, ten leaders of Ahl Hisan tribe of Gurmat Beni Saīd, the traditional enemy of Beni Isad, came at dawn one day shrouded in white winding sheets, and claimed sanctuary in the guest house of the shaikh. Each man tied himself to a pillar of the guest house and demanded death or peace. They were forgiven and granted a truce, presented with clothes, and returned safely to their tribe. Had any one of these men been caught outside the guest house, he would have been savagely killed.

The responsibility for any insult or harm befalling anyone in the guest house must be shouldered by its owner. The offended person is expected to cease attending the guest house until its owner apologizes to him by sending a special delegation.

In the same way, those who commit grave crimes are never given coffee in a guest house. I mentioned earlier the exclusion of a man accused of incestuous relations with his daughter-in-law. An effective way of stirring the conscience or the manly pride of tribesmen and of challenging them, is to refuse them coffee in a guest house. The reason has to be stated and the challenged men will never attend that guest house until they have cleared their names. If there were inadequate grounds for the refusal to serve coffee, a man might ask reparation from the owner. During the days of Shaikh Salim Ahl Khayūn, the tribe of il-Muwajid, who were affiliated to Beni Isad, lodged a complaint with him against a neighbouring tribe, Albu Shama. The shaikh sent Hsain Ahl Iawaiti, a lineage headman, to warn the Albu Shama tribe not to cause the tribe of il-Muwajid any further trouble. But the Albu Shama tribe neither heeded the shaikh's messenger nor did they promise any better relations with the tribe of il-Muwajid. Hsain Ahl Iawaiti took their attitude as a grave insult to himself and to his shaikh and wanted Ahl Iawait, his own lineage, to avenge the insult alone. As soon as he arrived back at ech-Chibayish, he pounded his coffee and all the men of his lineage gathered in his guest house. He himself carried the coffee pot and going round the assembled men he served none of them with coffee. All the men were shocked and asked for the reason, and the answer came from Hsain: 'Who of you deserves coffee?' He then told them of the insult he had suffered. The men chanted their war songs and the whole Ahl Iawait lineage, followed by other warriors, went on the same evening to the Albu Shama tribe and on the following morning a battle took place in which the Albu Shama tribe was utterly defeated

THE ETIQUETTE OF THE GUEST HOUSE

The etiquette of the guest house shows clearly the esteem or even veneration in which it is held.

People who attend the guest house must come fully dressed, especially with the head rope ('agāl) and the outer cloak (bishit). They should not speak unless they are spoken to, especially if they are not of a high social status. Jokes and unnecessary laughter must be avoided, and in case of anger and disputes a tribesman must speak clearly and calmly. Anayid Ahl Mhammed, of Ahl ish-Shaikh clan, had constant trouble with his two sons, who used to quarrel frequently. One early morning they quarrelled and so angered their father that he hurried to ask the intervention of the șirkal. In his anger he went to the clan guest house without wearing his head rope. When he lodged his complaint he was unable to control himself enough to speak clearly. The șirkal listened to him very coldly, and when Anayid finished, he blamed him strongly for attending without a head rope and talking confusedly. Then the șirkal added insultingly, 'I thought that one of your old wives had run away with a lover.' Only a man who has been afflicted with great shame, such as the elopement of a wife, may attend a guest house without a proper head-dress, as he never wears it until he 'regains his honour'.

Etiquette is also a clear indication of social standing. Everyone who attends the guest house should sit in the place which corresponds to his social rank. People of high social status, such as *is-sāda*, Ahl Khayūn and *ajawīd it-tayfa*, sit in the place of honour, which is usually distinguished by carpets and pillows. Social status is shown by the distance at which a tribesman sits from this place of honour, which is in the middle of the guest house by the hearth where coffee is brewed in winter, and near one of the two doorways in the summer.[1] The guest house owner can show his respect to an esteemed visitor or to a stranger, by personally leading him or showing him to his proper place, offering him a cigarette, or by ordering tea to be prepared and served to him as well as the usual coffee.

When entering the guest house and passing the first assembled tribesmen, the newcomer says '*As-salāmu 'alaykum*' ('peace be with you'), to which all must answer, '*Wa 'alaykum is-salām*' ('And peace may be with you') or with one or more additional sentences according to the status of the newcomer.

The assembled people must show their respect to every newcomer according to his social status. A man must rise to his feet to those who are higher in rank than himself. For instance, all members of the commoner and the slave classes rise to those of the three higher ranks. One of the criteria of social standing of a *khayir* (good fellow) is *ila koma bil muḍīf* (lit. = 'to him there is a standing in the guest house'). According to the difference in rank between the persons already assembled and the newcomer, the act of rising itself varies from rising fully to the feet and standing respectfully until the newcomer is seated, to a mere gesture, sometimes no more than raising the hips a few inches from the ground.

When the new arrival is comfortably seated, every man in the guest house should salute him by saying '*ṣabbaḥkum allah bil-khair*' ('May God make your morning good'), and he should answer every one with the same sentence, standing or affecting to stand in answering those of the people of higher social status than himself. This complicated system of salutation, the failure to comply with which is taken as a serious lapse of good manners, becomes very confusing when people arrive in groups of threes and fours, and standings, sittings and salutations have to be performed quickly and accurately. One has to be quick-witted to act in full conformity with tribal convention.

Whenever food is served in guest houses on occasions such as a feast, marriage or funeral ceremonies, it is the tradition that the owner should invite every man present to eat. Since there are usually too many men to sit and eat at one time, food is laid on the floor and men called to eat in two or three groups, one after the other. Here the principle of ranking emerges again. As all participants are supposed to wash their hands before taking the meal, the owner or his younger brother or son, or perhaps a slave, goes round the assembly carrying a pitcher and basin. The owner invites

---

[1] The tradition of Ahl Khayūn chiefs is to sit against the third pillar on the right-hand side in summer, and against the seventh in winter.

everyone to wash his hands. He begins with the men of the highest social standing, a *sayyid* or *mūman*, and proceeds to men of lower status. If he happens to neglect someone or puts one man before another wrongly, he is corrected by those whom he tries to rank in a higher position. If another man carries the basin and pitcher, the owner announces the names and the washing of hands goes accordingly. When the first group is called to eat the owner must invite them personally and must see that the principle of social ranking is accurately applied. When the first group finish eating, the second group is called and more food may be brought if the remains are thought to be insufficient. Second servings lack the delicacies served for the first group. Again it is the tradition that the man of the highest social ranking should set aside the coffee and food for the coffee-man of the guest house, before starting to eat.

We have seen in the previous chapter that there is mobility between two sub-classes, the *ṣirkals*, *mukhtārs* and *ajawid it-tayfa* and the ordinary commoners. This mobility is demonstrated in the guest house etiquette. Those commoners who approach the status of *ajawid it-tayfa* are given better places and more ceremonial respect. A *ṣirkal* or one of *ajawid it-tayfa* who, by his own misdeeds or those of his family, realizes that he has lost prestige, will take the initiative in seeking a lower place and no-one will prevent him. Again, a commoner, for instance, would gain more respect and be seated in a better place after returning from a pilgrimage or a visit to one of the tombs of the Imams.

Formal social stratification may be complicated by age-status. An old slave may sit in a better place than a younger commoner, especially if he is known to be *khayir* (good fellow). Similarly, a younger *sayyid* or Khayūni may sit in a lower place than that of an old *ṣirkal* or *mukhtār*. It is important to mention that *is-sāda* are in most cases not allowed to take a lower place than their usual one, as respect to them is a religious duty. In the guest house of Ahl ish-Shaikh clan the sessions are presided over by Abdil Hadi Ahl Khayūn, a very old Khayūni chief, according to the principle of respecting the elder strictly followed by Ahl Khayūn. A younger Khayūni member sits well away from the elder member, though in doing so, he sits very much lower than his social standing in relation to the other guest demands. If an old Khayūni member leaves, a younger Khayūni member who has been sitting in a lower place may take his rightful place, indeed the others urge him to do so. But if a Khayūni went alone to a guest house, he would be seated in the best place regardless of his age.

The tribesmen know these rules and adhere to them strictly. Everyone knows the exact standing of everyone else and treats him accordingly. Particularly if he had been for some reason an irregular attender at guest house meetings, a man might out of politeness or humility take a lower place than was his by right, but the owner, or those whom he has made to sit unduly higher than himself, would urge him to move to his correct place. Quite often, when such a man insists on sitting in a lower place than his social status requires, those who fail to persuade him to sit in a higher place, may correct their false position by changing their own places and sitting lower in relation to him.

Coffee is served in a little cup and each guest is offered three cups. Those who feel satisfied after the first or second cup can decline by shaking their empty cups to the coffee-man. People of high social status may be offered any number of cups till they decline by shaking them. The owner may honour a certain guest of rank, or a stranger, by asking his coffee-man to serve him with another round of coffee an hour or so after he has taken his first.

Those who commit mistakes, whether consciously or unconsciously, are corrected either directly by the *şirkal* or through a brother or a friend. If any tribesman deliberately infringes convention he may be checked and even dismissed from the guest house by the *şirkal*.

This rigid system of etiquette does not operate with the same accuracy in the smaller guest houses of the lineage headmen or notables, especially if the assembled people are few and all of the same lineage or neighbour-hood and therefore on familiar terms. Even in the large clan guest houses when the people of rank have left, and only a few people remain, the atmos-phere changes perceptibly to one of easy informality.

The interpolation of this very lengthy discussion of a single feature of Beni Isad culture may have struck some readers as both disproportionate and out of place; but it has, nevertheless, a very definite point. For the floor of the guest house may truly be called the stage upon which are con-tinually dramatized and reinforced the system of moral values, the social order and the close interlocking between them which has become apparent during the preceding chapters. In short, the guest house is a key insti-tution in the working of ech-Chibayish society.

PART THREE

Economic Organization

8

Agriculture

LAND TENURE

UNTIL the end of the nineteenth century, the various tribal groups and confederations in this part of Iraq held no fixed areas of land; and it was in an effort to increase political stability and central control that, about 1880, the Ottoman government declared the whole region State Domain, thereby forcing its inhabitants either to buy titles (*ṭāpū*) to fixed tracts of land, or to rent plots direct from the State.

The greater part of the lands involved, including those cultivated by the Beni Isad, were bought up by Ahl Sadūn, a powerful family who were suzerains of the confederation formed by Beni Isad and other tribes. As a result of the immense rents which Ahl Sadūn then attempted to impose on their subordinate shaikhs, the authorities—at that time British—again intervened. They ordered occupants of all disputed lands forthwith to pay rent directly to the State, promising the former Sadūn landlords compensation should the findings of an investigation into the disputes be in their favour. (The investigation, incidentally, is still incomplete.)

So far as Ahl ech-Chibayish were concerned, the result was that during the last years of the old regime, the Khayūni shaikhs paid rent to the State for the greater part of the land cultivated by the village, sub-letting in their turn to the *fellahīn*. Finally, on the abolition of the shaikhdom, each *ṣirkal* was made the lessee of the land cultivated by his clan, sub-letting it in turn to clansmen and a few fellow tribesmen from other clans. In addition to the lands thus leased from the State, there remained a few plots held by individuals under *ṭāpū* titles, purchased on various occasions through the years; but these were a tiny minority.

These changes in the form of land tenure were accompanied, among the Beni Isad, by great changes in the amount of land under cultivation. The history of Beni Isad in ech-Chibayish region shows that they had cultivated a large area of their enemies' lands in il-Mijarra, Amara and li-Hwaiza districts for varying periods. However, towards the close of the last century and after the defeat of Shaikh Hasan Ahl Khayūn by the Ottoman army, all Beni Isad retreated to the sanctuary of ech-Chibayish. They gave up the rich lands of Obū Ijaj, il-Abid, li-Hmaila, li-Awaidiya, etc., and utilized a much smaller area of hitherto uncultivated land in the vicinity of ech-Chibayish. In these new conditions, under which winter cultivation almost disappeared and summer cultivation could be carried out only occasionally, owing to successive floodings, mat-weaving was adopted as a means of livelihood, thus making cultivation less vital.

It follows that in ech-Chibayish land tenure is relatively unimportant, as cultivable land is not the main means of livelihood. A brief summary of the main types of rights to land is therefore sufficient.

There are two main legal forms of tenure; private ownership, obtained by the purchase of a land registration certificate, *ṭāpū*, as described above, and lease of State Domain. Only one small plot is to-day held by a private *ṭāpū* title-holder. The effective holders of the State Domain land are for the most part, the *ṣirkals*, who may lease these lands, on the *naqsha* system, by which the user has a right to prescriptive ownership after a given period. The *ṣirkal* has a right to one-third of the crops, and the user cannot be evicted unless he has failed to cultivate or to pay the *ṣirkal's* share. He can sell his right of occupancy, and mortgage or share his land. This system is usual when the *ṣirkal* leases land to members of his own clan.

The cultivating unit is usually the family. Sometimes two or more families, usually of one lineage, cultivate jointly, sharing the seeds and the crop. Frequently, a lineage may cultivate jointly. If so, they may share according to the number of *habil*[1] cultivated by every family, the money spent and the crop produced. Clans tend to hold adjacent patches of land, usually near their dwelling islands. In the days of the feudal shaikhdom, the lineages received land direct from the shaikh and no doubt their corporate solidarity was derived from this as well as from other institutions. To-day lineages or clans (except one) have no corporate rights to land. Inheritance is from father to son.

Land disputes, which may arise over boundaries or claims for rights of utilization, can be dealt with by the *ṣirkals* if both contesting parties are his clansmen, and he may resort to the *ajawid* of the clan for advice. If, however, the dispute involves different clans, or is between two *ṣirkals*, it is settled by the government, by arbitration.

There are large areas of land which cannot be cultivated because of floods, both around ech-Chibayish, south of the river Euphrates, and on the southern edge of Hor il-Hammar. These lands are either held by the *ṣirkals* or are unallocated State Domains. Most produce extensive belts of reeds and bulrushes. Some patches of land in or beyond the southern edge of Hor il-Hammar have a rich growth of grass.

LAND AND WATER

High flood waters cover all the cultivable land from March to August, except in rare years when they recede in July. As wheat and barley, the profitable crops, must be cultivated in the winter between January and April, they are out of the question in this region.

The only possible cultivation is therefore that of late summer crops,

[1] *habil* = 2·5 decores or 0·62 acres.

such as rice and great millet, raised from young seedlings of 30 to 45 days, which are transplanted from other areas less susceptible to flooding. In years of prolonged flooding, the water does not recede before August, and no cultivation is possible. There was none at all, for example, for five years from 1934 to 1938, and only very late and scanty cultivation during 1940. There was none in 1941, 1945, 1946, 1950 and 1953. Cultivation has thus been possible in only ten of the last 20 years. It is uncertain and unprofitable since it depends on the chances of water recession, and is confined to very late crops which have a low yield. Ahl ech-Chibayish say that they do not cultivate for profit but because they are hungry.

Some of Ahl ech-Chibayish have begun recently to migrate to the Amara region in order to cultivate there, and to return with enough food for their families for a few months. This migration, however, is not widespread. Not more than 50 families migrated in 1953. Many families have given up altogether the uncertainties of cultivation and prefer to depend entirely on reed-gathering.

During the 1952 agricultural season, in a sample of 120 families, 50 families (41·7%) did not cultivate at all; while only 70 families (58·3%) depended on cultivation alone, 40 (33·3%) supplemented cultivation with mat-weaving, and 21 (17·5%) supplemented cultivation with other occupations. The nine families who depended on cultivation alone were able to do so because they cultivated early crops outside ech-Chibayish.

In the agricultural season of 1952, only 113 *habil* were cultivated by the 70 families, the average area cultivated per family being only 1·6 *habil* (1 acre). To give an idea of the amount of uncultivable land compared with cultivable land, I calculate that the *şirkal* of Ahl ish-Shaikh clan held 13 plots, totalling over 12,000 *habil* in area. Of this, 11,000 *habil* were uncultivable (88%), and 1,400 cultivable.

CROPS

The only crops cultivated at ech-Chibayish are paddy rice (*oryza sativa*) and great millet (*sorghum vulgare*). Rice is more difficult to cultivate than great millet, needing irrigation and special care, while its seedlings are more expensive: it is therefore cultivated less. All the rice produced at ech-Chibayish is consumed locally, while nearly half the great millet is exported, mainly to Basra. As the *fellahin* are compelled to pay their debts in crops, and as the majority of them are in debt, a large proportion of the crop accumulates in the hands of the few moneylenders, who export the surplus. In addition, some of the *fellahin* sell all or part of their share of the crop because of urgent need for cash. This is why, although ech-Chibayish imports cereals for its own consumption, there is an export of millet. For example, the approximate tonnage of export of great millet was in 1949 240 tons, in 1951 220 tons, and in 1952 120 tons. Traders estimate that between 100 and 150 tons of rice, and between 200 and 250 tons of great millet are consumed annually at ech-Chibayish.

Both these crops are staple foods, but as great millet is the cheaper and more plentiful it is more widely consumed. The price of both crops fluctuates during the year. In 1952 the prices per *mann*[1] were:

	During harvest season	Six months later	Before the next season
Rice	ID 2/000	ID 2/500	ID 3/250
Great millet	ID 1/800	ID 2/250	ID 2/500

SOIL PREPARATION AND PLANTING

The soil of ech-Chibayish is mainly loam, and of great potential fertility. It is porous and friable, and fairly free of sterilizing salts. The presence of a large amount of lime in the soil makes it easy to work, and there is a considerable quantity of fine sand which is an advantage for drainage and washing.

Most of the land at ech-Chibayish is covered by bulrushes which must be cut before cultivation, either in April before the water rises very high, or in June when it begins to recede.

Although the *fellahin* recognize the value of ploughing, they rarely do it, since it costs about 600 *fils* per *habil*, and cultivation is not usually sufficiently profitable for such an outlay. Consequently the proportion of ploughed land is very low, probably not exceeding 5 per cent of the total cultivated land. Patches once ploughed are left for many years before they are ploughed again.

Ploughing is done by a native plough, *fidaān*, which is drawn by oxen, cows or men, or alternatively, the land may sometimes be dug with the long-handled spade. Both ploughing and digging take place immediately after the harvest, because land is much improved if it is worked before being inundated.

Seed-beds are rare, because in most years the floods do not recede in time. Only great millet seed-beds are sometimes sown; and the majority of the seedlings are brought from il-Mijarra.

During the 1952 agricultural season rice seedlings cost between 200 and 300 *fils* per 100 bundles and great millet seedlings 150 to 200 *fils* per 100 bundles.

Some *fellahin*, who cannot secure sufficient money to buy seeds, go to il-Mijarra and lease patches of land to sow rice; the rent paid is usually one-third of the shoots. This is a cheaper and better way of getting seeds, but it requires migration for a month or more to il-Mijarra.

When the *fellahin* transplant their seeds they do not live in the fields, which are outside the village, but a month later when the crop is high they move to their fields for about two months till the end of the harvest and crop division. Those who cultivate in places where reed is accessible, take all their families and continue mat-weaving in the intervals of farm work, whilst those who farm in places far from reed sometimes leave some of

---

[1] *mann* = 90 kilograms or 198 lbs.

their womenfolk at home to continue mat-weaving. Most of the *fellahīn* take with them all their cattle and belongings and every family usually takes three pairs of ready-made reed pillars, and some large mats for each temporary hut. Both great millet and rice require about 120 days from sowing to harvest.

IRRIGATION

Great millet does not need irrigation; the drier the land, the better the yield. Rice, however, is only cultivated on the banks of rivers or larger streams, since it depends on the tide for irrigation and drainage. *Fellahīn* make low earth dams on the water side and others to landward. If the land needs irrigation a breach is made in the water-side dam during the tide, and when sufficient water has flowed in the breach is closed. When surplus water has to be drained off, the other dam is breached during the ebb. If some patches get insufficient water, it is carried to the field in a *nazūḥa*, a little shallow basket with ropes, handled by two persons. This is not necessary more than once a week for four or five weeks.

HARVEST

Rice is harvested with a curved-handled sickle, whilst the great millet is harvested by hand. The rice and great millet ears are brought to a *maḥalla* for threshing and winnowing. The rice ears are piled in heaps about nine feet high, arranged in circles, with the ears towards the centre, leaving an opening to expose the ears to the air. For great millet, a patch of land is cleaned and beaten flat and the ears spread out on it.

Great millet can be threshed by beating or by treading animals. Threshing by beating is preferred as the grains are then cleaner. It is carried out with long sticks made of the frond midribs of date palms. Teams of two or three sit facing one another and beat the crop. Payment is in kind, $\frac{1}{24}$ of the crop. Threshing by animals is easier for the *fellahīn* but not more than 20 per cent of the great millet yield is threshed in this way. The animals used are cattle and sometimes donkeys hired from outsiders who happen to be near the fields. The usual payment for threshing by animals is 5 per cent of the crop threshed. Rice is threshed by animal treading. A layer of the crop is put down and the animals, with their muzzles tied, are driven over it.

Winnowing of both crops is usually carried out by women, dropping the grain and chaff to the ground from shallow baskets raised over their heads. Men use a winnowing fork or an ordinary paddle. The *fellah* can do the threshing himself or employ another, but in both cases payment is drawn from the produce before division.

After the crop is divided, both the landholders and *fellahīn* transfer their shares[1] to their homes by canoes or boats. The *fellah* is not responsible for transferring the landholder's share to the village, but if asked he does so

[1] This term is explained on p. 84.

G

willingly. Most of the *fellahīn* have their own canoes in which they return home with both their temporary huts and what crop is left for themselves.

The *akhaḍar* moneylenders and local traders keep in close contact with the *fellahīn* during the harvest either to get their loans repaid, or to buy from needy *fellahīn* while prices are low.

CROP DIVISION

When the crop is threshed and winnowed, the rice is piled in a long heap facing east and west. At the west, either a dagger[1] is thrust into the heap or a *turba*[2] is placed over it. This is believed to increase the crop 'by the will of God' and to put God's blessing upon it. The great millet cannot be piled in heaps because it must be kept aired and so no dagger is used.

When the crop is ready for division the landholder or his representative is present. The division is carried out either by a shallow basket, which usually holds two *wijia* (7½ Kg.), or by a balance. In the first case a measurer is employed, who faces the direction of Mecca, fills his basket and empties it by throwing it backward, over his shoulders. The measurer receives as payment one basketful per heap measured. When the crop is divided by weight, a weigher, who receives one *raf'ad* (lift) for each heap, must be employed. The lift is also two *wijia* (7½ Kg.). Division by weight is preferred when there is selling on the spot, so that the crop can be divided and weighed in one process.

Certain portions of the crop are subtracted from the gross production of the field before the final division.

Firstly, the *fellah* and all members of his family who are actually living in the field may consume any amount of the crop. In addition, he may barter part of the crop for fish, dates or dairy products, and even tea, sugar and tobacco, if there is a shop in the vicinity, using the fruits of his barter for family consumption. He cannot barter the crop for items other than food. This can go on from the time at which the crop is edible until it is divided. Though this is not openly approved, all the *fellahīn* practise it, and the landholders are quite aware of it; but the *fellah* is not allowed to pay his debts from the crop till after the division.

Secondly, about 5 per cent of the crop is given as wages for the threshing and if the *fellah* threshes for himself, he takes the wage before the division.

Thirdly, there are the wages of division, which have been described above.

Finally, one basket called *chelat il-ism allāh*[3] must be put aside to be

---

[1] The dagger symbolizes il-Abbas's sword, a ritual feature.

[2] *Turba* is a little round or square piece of dried mud, supposed to be made from the clay of the spot on which Imam Lihsain was killed at the battle of Karbala. The Shi'ah sect of Islam put a *turba* between their foreheads and the ground in prostration for prayers.

[3] *Chelat il-ism allāh* literally means 'the basket of in-the-name-of-God'. Moslems are inclined to open any important act in which they seek the blessing and mercy of God by saying *bism-illa hir-raḥman ir-raḥim* (in the name of God, the compassionate the merciful). Every verse of the *Qur'ān* is preceded by this sentence.

given either to a needy *sayyid* or to a poor person. This act is supposed to bring the blessing of God and the increase of the future crops.

The *fellah* is not responsible to the landholder for theft of the crop by outsiders before the division, but the landholder may make an inquiry and if there is evidence that the *fellah* himself, or his kin, have taken part in the theft, the landholder could compel the *fellah* to pay back the stolen crop. If the *fellah* presents an unreasonably small quantity of crop, the landholder can ask him to take an oath that he has not stolen any, and will probably not grant him land to cultivate the next year.

The *fellah* has the right to take any quantity of the great millet stems after harvest, for cattle-fodder, and can even give some to his kin or friends. The rest is sold by the landholder, usually to the *Ma'dan* who come to the region every winter. The average price of the stems is ID 1/000 per *habil*. The rice stems are not sold in ech-Chibayish. The *fellah* usually takes what he requires, sends some to the landholder, and leaves the rest in the field.

Sometimes, in conformity with the ideals of generosity, the landholder is expected to give up his entire share in the crop of some of those who cultivate his land, and to take only part of his share from others.

Though the division is supposed to be on a fixed basis it differs in practice considerably, according to the relation between the clan and the *şirkal* and to other personal factors.

VEGETABLE CULTIVATION

Vegetable cultivation at ech-Chibayish is a despised occupation and therefore not practised. All the vegetables eaten by the villagers are either brought from Basra or are grown by strangers called *ḥasawiya*, in the village itself or its outskirts.

A few families of *ḥasawiya* come to ech-Chibayish immediately after the floods have gone down and hire the few uninhabited islands or patches of land for the season, from September to November. During these three months they cultivate many varieties of vegetable, such as radish, lettuce, tomatoes, cucumber and so on, and sell them at the village market.

DATE PALMS
(*Phoenix dactylifera* Linn.)

According to the calculation of the Iraqi Board of Dates in 1951, there were 15,047 palms at ech-Chibayish, the annual output of which was 274,346 kilograms of dates. The number of date palms is decreasing because successive floods and high waters are destroying more palms than the inhabitants are able to plant. Many people assured me that there used to be more date palms than there have been during the last ten years.

The number of date palms that have survived is probably the result of the unusually low water which occurred in several successive years before 1935 and allowed five- or six-year-old young palms to become sufficiently deep-rooted to withstand the high waters which came later. Many palms fell during the last flood season. In the low-water season a low foundation of earth held by matting, six to eight feet in diameter, is built around the young or weak date palm to protect it from being washed away by water. Nearly all the date palms are owned by the families on whose dwelling islands they stand. But there are two exceptions; some families own groves of palms on uninhabited islands, and others own date palms on islands inhabited by others. On an average, each family owns about ten date palms, though some have none.

In 1953 the palm-owners of ech-Chibayish began to harvest their dates from 20 August onwards, and towards the end of the month the harvest was at its peak. Towards the end of the first week of September nearly all the date palms were harvested. When the date is partly ripe, small quantities are occasionally gathered to be consumed by the owners. This partial and occasional harvest continues till all the dates of the palm are fit to be cut.

The average annual yield of a date palm is probably between 70 and 120 pounds. The fruit which remains after the occasional gathering, and the depredations of birds, is preserved to be sold or consumed later during the year.

Nearly all the yield of the date palms is consumed in ech-Chabiyish itself. Every palm-owning family cuts, cooks and preserves its own dates, and sells them, either preserved in baskets or cooked, to the village traders who sell them again in the village shops. The prices of the cooked varieties during 1953 were between ID 2/250 and ID 3/000 per *mann* and the preserved baskets between 500 *fils* and 750 *fils* per basket, according to the quality of the date. In a few cases, the whole yield of one palm is sold before ripening for between 200 and 350 *fils*, and the buyer is free to come at any time and collect the dates.

Ahl ech-Chibayish use the other products of the date palm in various ways. The trunk is used for bridges and in building large huts and guest houses. It is sometimes used as fuel for coffee fires. The fronds and frond bases are used for fuel; and the leaflets of the fronds are woven into baskets and fans. The date palms of ech-Chibayish are too precious to be felled deliberately for any purpose, but trunks of palms are used or sold, when fallen, and the fronds and their bases are cut off the palms each year after the harvest.

LIVESTOCK

Cattle are the only livestock kept in ech-Chibayish, though a few sheep are brought to the village from time to time for sale to the only butcher there, or to those who wish to offer a sheep as a mourning or marriage gift. Sheep cannot be bred in the village because of lack of pasture. Ahl ech-Chibayish are not buffalo-breeders though they realize how profitable it is. They argue that 'we are not Ma'dan to take up such an occupation'. Besides, buffalo-keeping would compel them to leave ech-Chibayish and live on artificial floating platforms in the Hor, and they are reluctant to do this. Six of the seven people of ech-Chibayish who own buffaloes keep their beasts outside the village, in the care of Ma'dan living in the Hor. The remaining owner can keep his single buffalo on his island because it is situated on the outskirts of the village. As buffaloes are strong and fierce, they have to be kept on separate floating platforms rather than on the islands of the village where they would damage the huts and the date palms, or cause inconvenience by wading through the narrow waterways. Buffaloes also need great attention; their care is a full-time occupation which forces their owners to abandon any other means of earning a living. Ahl ech-Chibayish are now specialized as mat-weavers and cultivators; some of them migrate for long periods every year, and consequently they cannot take up the full-time task of buffalo-keeping. The seven buffalo owners own 84 head altogether; one owns 30 buffaloes, two 20 head each, and the remaining four owners own 14 head between them. For the care of the buffaloes, the Ma'dan demand from the owners all the dairy produce and half the offspring. Though they cannot benefit from their produce, the owners keep the buffaloes, mainly as a reserve of wealth, selling one or two of them in times of need.

The cattle kept in ech-Chibayish are slightly humped, small, yellow in colour and very mild in temper. Their number has been estimated at about 4,500 head. Out of the sample of 120 families studied in detail there were 79 families owning cattle; in only nine families were there more than five head of cattle; 16 families owned one each.

The possession of cattle does not confer prestige. No value, other than their market price, is attached to them. On the contrary, the attempt to acquire cattle, like any attempts to acquire personal economic advantage, may help to lower the owner's prestige. Cattle are not normally used in marriage payments, but can be given as a substitute for a proportion, if the bride's father agrees.

Cattle are valuable both as a reserve of wealth and as a source of food. Ahl ech-Chibayish do not part with an animal easily, but when compelled to pay shares of compensation, marriage payments, or debts, they may have to sell one or more cows. In 1953, the current prices of cattle[1] at ech-Chibayish were:

	Young	Medium-sized	Full-grown
Cow	ID 3/ooo	ID 10/ooo	ID 13/ooo
Ox	ID 2/ooo	ID 3/ooo	ID 5/ooo

The greatest value of the cattle lies in their dairy products. Fresh and sour milk, butter and curds are prized foods.

Ahl ech-Chibayish take great care of their cattle. For about eight

[1] The prices of buffalo are about double the prices of cattle and a good milch buffalo may fetch as much as ID 30/ooo.

months of the year stock is confined to the little islands and fodder is
brought to them daily by children or women. For about four months, in
the low-water season, the cattle are taken away from the dwelling islands
by small boys and girls to graze on the nearest patches of land. Sometimes
the animals themselves wade the waterways in search of pasture. The permanent fodder for cattle are the rushes, and the young green reeds. When
cultivation takes place, stalks of rice, and of great millet, are stored for
feed when the usual fodder becomes scarce or grows a long way from the
village.

During the winter months, cattle are kept in temporary byres which are
rebuilt every year. When the weather gets warm and the byre is worn out,
it is dismantled and the cattle are left in the open air or given access to a
deserted dwelling hut. Unlike the other Marsh Dwellers, Ahl ech-Chibayish never keep their cattle inside their own dwelling huts. Women look
after the byres and both dung and dirty fodder are removed every day.
Cattle are watered twice daily during the hot season and once during the
cold season.

Cattle-owners in ech-Chibayish never stated exactly how much milk
their cows yielded, but a milch cow may yield more than 20 pints per day,
excluding what is left for her calf, the majority of cows giving between 10
and 15 pints. It is believed that someone with the evil-eye would harm a
cow with a good milk yield if this became known; and cattle-owning
families rarely give presents of milk or other dairy products lest the exact
yield of their herd should be disclosed.

Milk is consumed daily, but families who own a large number of cows
have a surplus of milk which is turned into clarified butter and kept for
family consumption. Very few families sell clarified butter to the village
shops because selling butter is despised as a Ma'dan occupation. The
majority of cattle-owning families turn their milk into curds to be eaten
with bread or boiled rice, or churned into buttermilk and butter. Buttermilk is drunk with meals and butter is either eaten fresh or preserved after
being clarified. The other varieties of dairy products, such as cream and
cheese, are not produced by Ahl ech-Chibayish but are frequently sold in
the village by Ma'dan women.

Ahl ech-Chibayish never slaughter a cow deliberately for meat, but
they may slaughter cattle and eat the meat in certain circumstances. If a
cow or an ox is ill, the owner hastens to slaughter it, as the consumption of
its flesh would be tabooed for religious reasons if the animal were to die a
natural death. He sells the meat, distributing some of it as gifts to kin and
neighbours. In times of trouble or for the fulfilment of a wish, Ahl ech-
Chibayish may promise to sacrifice a calf to Allah or one of the Imams.
When the trouble is past or the wish fulfilled, the animal is sacrificed and
its meat distributed among the poorer families and members of the lineage,
but never sold.

When one of Ahl ech-Chibayish builds a guest house, especially a clan guest house, a calf is slaughtered, if the number of workers is large, on each of the two big occasions of building. Meat is not regarded as a normal item of diet. Anyone not invited to a meal containing meat may not taste it for years. The only butcher in the village sells the meat to the village officials, teachers and the few traders and shopkeepers who can afford to buy it. A poor man seen carrying half a pound of meat may well be asked by his friends, 'What is the trouble? Which of your family is ill?', because it would instantly be assumed that one of his family was in desperate need of good nourishment.

The difficulty of providing sufficient pasture for eight months of the year, for animals kept on the islands, makes cattle-tending a tiresome task, especially during the cold months. Moreover, it is not easy to keep more than a few cows on a small island. Factors such as these restrict cattle-raising at ech-Chibayish.

Tribal traditions also prevent cattle from being a regular source of income, as selling dairy products is despised. Consequently, the people who have no cattle buy what dairy products they need for their diet from canoe-shops run by Ma'dan women, and those who have a surplus of milk can do no better than consume it extravagantly at home. But for this traditional ban, the non-cattle-owning families could have cheaper dairy products and the cattle-owning people might earn a regular income.

9

Other Subsidiary Occupations

'HAD it not been for the reed, all the people would have left ech-Chibayish.' This statement is often heard in ech-Chibayish, especially when cultivation is prevented by inundation and the mat trade becomes the only source of livelihood. Although from the viewpoint of the outsider, ech-Chibayish offers little obvious attraction to its inhabitants, they themselves do not like the idea of emigration and of living elsewhere as 'strangers'. Elsewhere Marsh Dwellers living under far better conditions have emigrated in great numbers, but Ahl ech-Chibayish have never totally abandoned their village.

The reason is almost certainly their tribal loyalty. The strong tribal solidarity felt by members of Beni Isad till recently may be the result of a long period of unification under the military leadership of Ahl Khayūn. Ahl ech-Chibayish believe strongly that they would be liable to humiliation or abasement if they were to live in small immigrant groups among other tribes or communities. They answer in bewilderment if asked why they do not migrate: 'How can I leave my brothers and my father's brothers to go and live among strangers? I would never change one reed of ech-Chibayish for a whole town.' After Shaikh Salim had been given land in Diyala province he tried repeatedly to induce some of Ahl ech-Chibayish to join him and cultivate on his vast estate. None of them agreed to do so, though he offered every *fellah* a large plot of land and cash in advance in an area where both winter and summer cultivation were known to be highly profitable. A few families did in fact migrate to il-Mijarra but they returned after three years though they had been cultivating successfully there and had made good profit.

Nevertheless, current conditions have caused seasonal and temporary migrations and long expeditions for hired labour and barter. I distinguish between migrations which usually last two to four months, and in which the whole family migrates, and expeditions which last only about two or three weeks. Fishing expeditions last about three months.

The three types of labour migration are the reed migration to Lishan from December till March; the harvest labour migration to il-Gharraf from April till June or August; and the date-packing migration from September to October.

THE REED MIGRATION TO LISHAN

Lishan is a large island about 250 yards in length and 100 yards in width. It is some three hours' paddling, about 15 miles, to the northeast of ech-Chibayish in the large thick reed belt which surrounds Bargat Bghadad lagoon. It can hold about 200 or more huts and even in the highest floods parts of it remain above water. This island seems to have been the site of an ancient city as it contains low mounds, buried bricks, and occasional pottery shards, beads and other archaeological remains.

There is evidence that Ahl ech-Chibayish have used this island for a long time. In military expeditions during the nineteenth century it served both as a military post and for habitation.

As the uncut reed is relatively inaccessible during the best (*jinība*) season, the families who are heavily in debt for mats prefer to live on Lishan in the midst of the reed belt to save constant journeys to and fro. During the last four or five years about 200 families have migrated to the island every year from December to March. During the winter of 1953 there were 208 families there: 123 of Ahl ish-Shaikh, 73 of il-Hadadiyīn and 12 of Beni Aschiri.

Since it is in connection with mat-weaving and does not involve hired labour, migration to Lishan is not despised: indeed, we have just shown that the majority of seasonal immigrants are Ahl ish-Shaikh, the clan with the highest prestige, who rarely take part in other migrations. As more families than the island can hold wish to migrate and work there, many try to migrate early in order to secure a place, building their huts on the highest point of the island. The immigrants erect small temporary huts of three arches each and thicken the walls with bulrushes and reeds to make them warm. The huts are built very close to one another with one broad thoroughfare dividing the island into two almost equal parts. They are erected as the families take up residence, beginning at the centre of the island, regardless of any clan or lineage grouping. There is no headman or chief in the community, and all the immigrants refer their disputes to their *şirkals* or to the government offices in ech-Chibayish.

There were four temporary shops on the island set up and run by four of the immigrants themselves. These shops sold and bartered flour, sugar, tea, tobacco, cigarette paper, salt, kerosene, and other less important articles such as thread, needles, tea-glasses, matches and so on. As barter is more profitable to the shopkeepers than sale, they preferred, like the in-Nazil shopkeepers, to have their goods bartered for mats for which they offered lower prices than in the village (often as little as 25 *fils*) and in return gave the immigrants goods both inferior in quality and dearer in price than those sold in the village market. These four shopkeepers acted as mat traders, not collectors, and made a considerable profit out of the mat trade during the four months of this migration. They followed the same procedure and policy as the in-Nazil shopkeepers and sold their mats to the mat traders of ech-Chibayish.

Apart from those bartered at the four shops, the mats produced at Lishan are given to one of the three mat collectors at Lishan or taken by the producers themselves to ech-Chibayish to be handed to a creditor or to be bartered or sold. The proximity of abundant reeds, and conditions which favour concentration on the weaving, raise the rate of production to more than double its average in the village. A family of four persons— husband and wife, a boy and a girl—can produce a daily average of 12 mats in an average working time of ten hours each for the adults and five hours each for the children.

Only those families who have strong reasons for facing hardships decide to migrate to Lishan. The majority of the 208 families were heavily in debt and went there in the hope that they would be able, after four months' hard work, to pay off their debts. All those in debt were able to pay back all or part of their debts, while the small number who were not, managed to save money.

THE HARVEST MIGRATION TO IL-GHARRAF REGION

Il-Gharraf region lies on both sides of the il-Gharraf river which flows from il-Kut to the Hor near Albu Salih. It is a vast, rich region where a great many winter crops are produced, so that in the harvest season the landholders need a large number of labourers to help gather the harvest in the shortest possible time. Hundreds of poor families from all the neighbouring districts migrate to work on il-Gharraf plantations as hired labourers. Though ech-Chibayish is a long way from il-Gharraf, being about 50 miles south of its southern border and more than 300 miles from its northern border, poverty drives many to migrate there for three or four months every year.

Emigrants leave the village at the beginning of April, as the early harvest commences about that time, and stay for periods ranging from two to four months, according to the tasks they perform. The majority of the emigrant families are of Ahl Ghrij clan. In 1953 180 families of the total number of ech-Chibayish emigrants, who were estimated at 250 families, were of this clan. The rest of the emigrants were of the Ahl Anaisi and Ahl Wais clans. It is significant that members of the other clans of Beni Isad do not migrate to il-Gharraf for months, but go several times by canoe to barter mats and reeds, occasionally hiring out their vessels. The higher the clan's prestige, the less its participation in this labour migration. The idea of working as labourers for others, and of exposing their womenfolk to undesirable conditions, deters the clans with higher prestige.

The emigrant families make preparations long before the migration. They borrow money to cover the extra expense of stocks of flour, sugar and tea, and the men put by bundles of reeds for barter and the construction of temporary huts on the plantations. Women of Ahl Ghrij clan weave a certain kind of basket in large quantities to sell in il-Gharraf where they are used for crop division.

As these poor families own no cattle and hardly any furniture except their simple bedding and some earthen and metal utensils, most of their possessions are taken with them in their canoes. They work anywhere they like, without contracts or agreements, and during the work they move at will. Before leaving the village a few families of one lineage may agree to travel and work together, but an agreement of this sort is not binding.

Arrived at their destination, the immigrants erect flimsy huts of two or three mats thrown over three arches of thin reed pillars. The landholder tells them where to pitch their huts.

The main task the labourers perform is harvesting. While the men are harvesting, their women carry heavy loads of stalks to be threshed and winnowed, and may take part in the latter. Where the crop has already been harvested, the women work as porters while the men use their boats, hiring them out to transfer the crop and to carry passengers. Meanwhile the baskets and reeds are bartered or sold by the women.

If the immigrants participate only in the harvest they return to their village as soon as it ends, about the end of May, thus staying only two months. If, on the other hand, they hire out their boats and find it more profitable or easier than working on plantations, they usually stay as late as August. As the majority of these emigrants cultivate summer crops at ech-Chibayish if the state of water permits, all those who wish to cultivate go back to the village before it is too late for summer crop cultivation. In 1953 when there was no summer cultivation, a small proportion of the emigrant families returned towards the end of June, the rest arriving at ech-Chibayish between 5 and 10 August.

Wages on the plantations are paid in kind, the average being a bundle of stalks as large as the labourer's arms can hold for the harvest of each *habil*. For winnowing and carrying, women receive a previously agreed quantity, about a *wijia* per day. Barley is always used for wages even if the crop harvested or winnowed is wheat. The labourers thresh and winnow their barley daily as they need it for meals, sometimes selling small quantities to grain-traders.

Out of the 120 families investigated there were 23 (19·2%) who migrated to il-Gharraf region in the season of 1953. Ten undertook only this one migration, while the remaining 13 families also migrated to Basra to work in date-packing stations. The profit made by the labourers from this migration seems to be very small. The net earnings of the 23 families until they got back to ech-Chibayish, excluding all expenses, was ID 125/000, an average of ID 5/434 per family for four months' work, the average family gain per month being only ID 1/358. The majority of the emigrants themselves stated that they usually do not gain more than their subsistence from such migrations, 'The food which fills our bellies', as they put it. Saving is beyond their expectations, and the majority felt they were fortunate to be able to return with one or two *mann* of barley.

The labourers are supposed to offer a share of the barley they have saved to their *sirkals*[1] on their return. Though there is no fixed rate, it is an almost established right for the *sirkal* to have at least a *wijia* in every *mann*. This share is called 'coffee for the guest house', i.e. a contribution to the expenses of the guest house.

THE DATE-PACKING MIGRATION

More than 200,000 tons of dates are exported every year from Iraq. They are packed in baskets, tins or wooden boxes at packing stations scattered along the Shatt il-Arab, the main centre of date production. As packing is done by hand, and has to be completed in two months, the packing stations need a large number of labourers during that period. Labourers' families from nearby districts on the Tigris and the Euphrates migrate to work in packing stations, and ech-Chibayish, like other marsh communities in the Hor il-Hammar region, supplies a large number.

The emigrant families leave ech-Chibayish in the first half of September. The number depends to a large extent on whether there is cultivation in that year, for in this event some families have to stay and look after their fields. Families who wish to migrate in the years when summer cultivation is possible can plant their shoots and leave one or more of their members to look after them, while the rest of the family are away. As the harvest usually takes place early in November, the emigrants can get back in time.

In 1953 285 families migrated. There were 248 families of Ahl Ghrīj, 24 of Ahl Anaisi, ten of Ahl ish-Shaikh and three of Ahl Wais clans. Here again the majority are of Ahl Ghrīj, the clan with the lowest prestige, while of Ahl ish-Shaikh the clan of the highest prestige, there were only ten families.

The date-packing carried out by women is more important than that done by men, who perform the duties of guards, porters, water-carriers and so on. The contracts between the packing companies and the agents are therefore based on the supply of women and not of men, who migrate mainly to accompany the women. In the season of 1953 over two-thirds of the migrants from ech-Chibayish were women.

The three agents who are responsible for supplying labourers from ech-Chibayish have contracts with two packing companies. Every January these three agents go to their packing companies to settle their accounts for the previous season and to make new contracts for the coming one. They give guarantees to fulfil their contracts.

The agent receives a sum of money, usually ID 500/000 for every 100 women hired, to be distributed among the labourers in two instalments. After receiving the first instalment, the agent returns to the village and settles his accounts with his labourers who have receipts for the work done during the previous season and are in debt to the agent for what they drew in cash or goods. At the same time he arranges new contracts and gives an

---

[1] The *sirkal* of Ahl ish-Shaikh is an exception. He neither asks for nor accepts any share other than his usual share from cultivation.

advance, about ID 3-5/000, to every woman who makes a new contract. On 15 August the agent advances his women labourers ID 1/000 each to cover travelling expenses. The agent charges the company 500 *fils* for each woman he supplies and 150 *fils* for each woman's or man's fare. This was originally supposed to be on the agent's account, but in fact he charges the labourers for their passage. In due course the agent hires one or two large sailing-boats and takes his labourers to the packing stations of the company for which he works. The immigrants take with them only the barest essentials, as the time they spend on this migration is short and the huts they live in are extremely small.

They erect huts either among the date palms near the packing stations or on a clear patch of land round the station. The huts are inconveniently small in size, light in construction, and afford little protection. They are used to store possessions and only occasionally to sleep in, since most labourers prefer to sleep in the open air. The agent has a large hut and an additional hut used as a guest house in which the expenses for the coffee and kerosene are borne by the company. He makes coffee every night after the evening meal and his labourers gather in his guest house to drink coffee and discuss the events of the day. The agent appoints a guard who watches the huts while the labourers leave the camp to work in the station during the day. Sick labourers do not receive any medical care or sick pay from the companies but they can get treatment individually at the government hospitals and dispensaries in the district. Sanitary conditions are bad in all three camps and stations.

The labourers eat bread and tea supplemented by occasional dates, meat, fish, curdled milk and onions which they buy from the nearby markets. They bake their bread in earthen ovens which they bring with them, or on earthen discs which they make themselves in the camps. The main foods are bought from the agent's stocks; and as the labourers usually have no cash, their advances having been spent before arriving at the camp, they find themselves compelled to buy from the agent, who sells to them on credit. His prices are about 10 per cent higher than at ech-Chibayish, and as he buys direct from wholesalers at Basra, his profit is rarely less than 30 per cent.

The majority of women from ech-Chibayish are employed in removing stones from the dates, the rate paid for stoning one type of box of net weight 42 lb. being 50 *fils*. Others arrange dates in other types of boxes at a rate of 30 or 31 *fils* per box; whilst a small proportion are engaged in selecting a certain quality of date suitable for packing in baskets and are paid 16 to 20 *fils* per basket. The minimum daily output of the women is two of the larger or three of the smaller boxes, which brings in roughly 100 *fils*; the maximum is four and six respectively, bringing in about 200 *fils*. Men doing the various minor jobs mentioned above receive monthly salaries ranging from ID 3/000 to ID 6/000.

The agents mulct the labourers of their wages by various methods. Besides holding the monopoly of the sale of provisions they cheat the labourers when they settle their accounts. The women, predominantly illiterate, receive only a portion of their daily wage in cash, getting a chit for what is often the greater part of their due; and later, when the time comes for settlement, they have no alternative but to accept any account the agents care to produce.

Moreover, the agents appropriate the salary of half the men employed by appointing only half the number of men previously agreed on with the company and compelling the men employed to do the work of the original number. To be fair to all the men present in their stations, the agents split them into two groups and make each group work only two weeks a month and receive half the monthly salary.

Out of 120 families of my census, 20 families migrated to the date-packing stations in the season of 1952. They were able to return to ech-Chibayish with total earnings of ID 179/500, the average earnings were ID 8/075 per family, and the monthly profit per family ID 4/387. Had it not been for exploitation by the agents, the profit would have been much higher.

In this account of labour migrations a number of points are to be emphasized. Only a small proportion of Ahl ech-Chibayish is involved in these movements—not more than 18 per cent of the village population at any one time; and the majority of the migrants are from Ahl Ghrīj clan.

In the reed migration to Lishan only 208 families migrated in the 1953 season, 13 per cent of the total number of ech-Chibayish families. In the migration to il-Gharraf region, only 250 families, 16·2 per cent of the total population of the village, took part. Of these 250 families, 72 per cent were of Ahl Ghrīj clan. In the date-packing migration, 285 families (17·8 per cent of ech-Chibayish families), of which 87 per cent were Ahl Ghrīj, migrated to the Basra region.

The gain from such migrations seems to be very small, except perhaps in the case of that to Lishan. Out of the il-Gharraf migration little more than subsistence for the period of migration was gained, and in the date-packing migration a high proportion of the returns was taken by the agents.

There would seem to be several good reasons why Ahl Ghrīj figure prominently in these movements. In the first place, having already a very low status in the community, they are uninhibited about following despised occupations; and secondly, as their inability to weave leaves them no means of filling the economic gap in years when flooding makes cultivation impossible, they are forced to emigrate to secure their mere subsistence.

FISHING

Fishing is carried out mainly by spearing and netting. Men and youths spear fish for their family meals in time left free from other occupations, going out at night in canoes to which lamps are attached as lures.

Only one technique of net-fishing is employed. This involves the use of a small circular net, the *silliya*, weighted with little balls of lead at the outer edge. The latter is thrown in such a way that it hits the water open in a complete circle; the weight of the lead then causes the edges to sink and finally to close, when the net is pulled up, so as to form a bag. During September a certain kind of small fish, called *khishni*, becomes abundant. The people of ech-Chibayish catch it by attracting it with lights so that it jumps into their canoes.

With another technique they take advantage of the fact that some migrating fish move with the current. They erect two low fences of bulrushes across the river; these meet at an obtuse angle, leaving a narrow opening, and stretch about ten yards from one bank of the river to its deeper part. At this narrow opening a small net is fixed and tied to a little bell. Big migrating fish may be carried between the two fences by the current. Trying to find the way out, a fish reaches the net, and struggles to free itself, thus making the bell ring. The waiting fisherman stuns the fish with a blow from a short stick, after which it is easily caught.

Boys also use a baited hook and line, which is usually fastened to a reed. A little cork or a piece of bulrush is used as a float.

About 150 men, mainly of Ahl Ghrīj clan, set out every year for a three-month fishing expedition in Hor il-Abid. The men are organized into groups of 10-18 men. The groups have no common leader or chief, each group leader managing his own group. When disputes occur, they refer to the police station at il-Abid or to their *sirkal* in the village.

The expedition takes place during February, March and April, when fish are plentiful in the Hor. Before setting out, a group of men agree to accept the leadership of one who can obtain the necessary money. The leader takes a loan, which may range from ID 150/000 to ID 180/000 from a moneylender, who acquires one share of the group for every ID 40/000 he lends. The leader then buys the net, which is about 400 yards in length, six yards in width and costs between ID 35/000 and ID 40/000. Then every three or four men form a sub-group, which brings provisions from the village and eats together. The group hires two or more sailing-boats, the owners of which receive one share for each boat hired. Two of the men well known for their skill and physical strength are appointed to perform special duties in the actual fishing and receive accordingly one and a half instead of one share each.

The fishing groups set out in sailing-boats with the necessary reeds for erecting temporary huts on il-Abid island, and with provisions and fishing implements. Each group erects a large hut and all build jointly a platform where the nets are spread and mended, together with another smaller platform for the roe to be washed and cleaned. The groups set out every day early in the morning, fishing separately, each group under its own leader. The Hor is divided into two parts, eastern and western, and half the groups fish in one part, changing over every day. The catch is split, sprinkled with salt and taken to be sold in Basra.

Every member of the group is given one fish a day for his evening meal, and every week or so, each sub-group sends a member to ech-Chibayish to bring flour, sugar, tea and tobacco. In addition, members of the group can draw money or provisions from their leader. They are made to pay an unlawful due to the policemen of il-Abid police station, consisting of nine fish per day for each fishing group. The *şirkal* of the clan of which the leader is a member charges them one share, and a present of about ID 1/000 or more at the end of the expedition as 'coffee for the guest house'; besides which some fish must be sent to him whenever a member of the group goes back to the village.

When the men return to the village the leader liquidates his accounts. The gross income is counted, and after all expenses for the net, salt, transport, the *şirkal's* presents and any other expenses are subtracted, the remainder is divided among the men as follows:

One share for every member of the group.
One share for the moneylender for every ID 40/000 given as interest in addition to the original money lent.
One share for the owner of each boat used by the group.
One additional share for the leader.
Two additional half-shares for the men with special tasks.
One share to the *şirkal* of the leader.

The share is handed over to each member after he has settled with the leader of the group all his debts in cash and kind, together with the money taken from the capital of the group before the expedition started. If a member has accumulated debts exceeding his share he has to work again the following year for the same leader, so that he may repay him. After the accounts have been settled, the net is cut into pieces and distributed among the members of the group.

During the 1953 season, 13 groups took part in the expedition. They were composed of 156 men, all of whom were of Ahl Ghrij clan except eight men from Ahl Anaisi clan. They worked 84 days. Seven groups borrowed capital sums of ID 160/000 each and the rest between ID 150/000 and ID 180/000. The net share of some groups was ID 5/600, others ID 7/300 and the share of one big and well organized group was about ID 11/000. 18 men (11·5 per cent) were found to have exceeded their shares before liquidation, 52 men (33·3 per cent) made between ID 1/000 and ID 3/000, and the remaining 86 (55·1 per cent) earned sums ranging from ID 4/000 to ID 7/500.

From my census of 120 families, I found that only 16 families altogether practised fishing. Of these, seven families fished by spearing and in all cases but one, the catch was not sold, but consumed. The only family fishing by the net method consumed all its catch.

Of the eight families who joined the expedition, one finished in debt; one earned about ID 7/000; six families earned between ID 4/000 and ID 5/000 each. The average profit of the seven families was ID 4/857 per family for the whole expedition.

Although fishing could be a profitable source of income, it is not widely practised. Except for Ahl Ghrij clan, Ahl ech-Chibayish never sell fish, because tribal traditions are against it. They prefer to spend time in mat-weaving, buying fish from outsiders if they desire it. Paradoxically, fish are extremely plentiful around the village, but a number of Ma'dan canoe-shops arrive there every day selling large quantities.

If all the clans of the tribe participated in fishing expeditions during the winter and in other fishing methods over the year, and if the catch were sold in the village and the surplus exported, fishing might be a valuable source of income. It would, moreover, provide the ech-Chibayish home market with fish at cheaper rates than the exhorbitant prices of the Ma'dan. Fish is the main relish for all ech-Chibayish, and great quantities are eaten daily in the village; yet because demand always exceeds supply, fish is sold for high prices all the year round.

FOWLING

The only hunting carried out in ech-Chibayish is fowling, limited to the winter season in December, January and February, and very few Ahl ech-Chibayish engage in it. There are, in fact, no more than 25 to 30 persons practising fowling and the bag is used almost exclusively for family con-sumption. Only two persons out of the 120 families in my census practised fowling for profit, one hunting by net-trap, the other with a gun. During the whole season of 1953 they made about ID 14/000 and about ID 8/000 respectively. The birds hunted are mainly coot and teal.

The same factors which limit fishing as a source both of food and of income operate here. People do not hunt because selling birds for profit is traditionally despised as a Ma'dan occupation. The large quantities of birds consumed during winter at ech-Chibayish are all bought from Ma'dan women. During winter birds are so plentiful and fowling is so easy that it might well be a very profitable employment if it were not restricted by tribal traditions.

H

Reed-Gathering and Mat-Making

ECH-CHIBAYISH is surrounded for many miles in all directions by reeds except, of course, in the south, where the old channel of the Euphrates runs. Just behind the river the reed beds begin again, in patches, though not so thick and continuous as the belt to the north of the village, which covers all the shallower marsh separating the river from the deeper water of Hor il-Hammar. The thick belt of reeds north and north-east of the village must be no less than 20 miles in depth, from north to south, and about 35 miles in length from east to west. This belt extends well across the boundaries of the village and even to the river in some parts. It contains a few open sheets of water and some deep lagoons, and is intersected by creeks, which though only a few yards in width are deep and navigable by canoes.

The reed (*Phragmites karka* Trin: Arabic *giṣab*) is a tall and thick variety. In the further beds such as Libmara and Obū Jene it grows 24 or even 30 feet above the surface of water. The average height is about 20 feet, and the average diameter between three and a half and four inches. Reeds grow so densely that a man or a narrow canoe cannot penetrate them.

Growth begins in January with the sprouting of soft green rushes, called locally *ḥashīsh* (grass); a little later, about April, they are called *angir*. In these two stages the reeds provide the best fodder for cattle and buffaloes. Then when they grow stout and high, but still green and soft, Ahl ech-Chibayish begin to cut them down and weave them into mats. At this stage the reed is called 'agga and is from 8 to 11 months old. When one year old it becomes thick, dry and yellow. Henceforth it is called *jinība* and is then most suitable for mat-weaving. Though it can live for a further two or three years, it is usually cut down after 18 months, when it is called *rubakh*, and is used only for fuel. Otherwise it is broken by winds as it gets thin and dry, and dies after about four years.

In order to secure better fodder for their herds, the Ma'dan burn the old reeds every year about January to make way for the younger rushes. This also benefits the mat-weavers, since it gives rise to young strong reeds. But as the burning is done at random, with no attempt to limit the fires, great quantities of good *jinība* reed are often destroyed, thus causing a temporary scarcity of reeds in certain districts.

REED-GATHERING TECHNIQUES

When the reed is at the green rush stage, it is abundant and accessible, not only in the immediate vicinity but even in the waterways of the village itself. Ahl ech-Chibayish prefer to gather the nearest reeds first, as fodder for their cattle. All the young green reeds in the waterways of the village and on the nearer creeks and watercourses disappear almost immediately. From February to August Ahl ech-Chibayish follow the growth of the 'angir and the younger 'agga, cutting down those nearest as fodder. Then they begin a search for the stouter 'agga which can be woven into mats. From the middle of August till the end of the year, they move out progressively further in search of reeds.

When the 'agga season ends, the available reeds lie at some distance from the village. From January till March there are usually two types of reed-gathering, the first for nearby rushes for cattle fodder, and the second for the more distant jiniba. It is at this season that some of Ahl ech-Chibayish migrate to a distant island in the heart of the marsh to get nearer to the reeds and thereby save long daily trips. In July and August the remaining jiniba are a greater and greater distance from the village and at the same time the young 'agga reed begins to mature; the long trips to gather jiniba reed are then gradually abandoned and from the middle of August mat-weavers rely entirely on the new reed. The natives continue to weave this 'agga from August to November. Thus, the reed-gathering trips differ according to the distance of the reed itself from the village.

Ahl ech-Chibayish undertake three types of trips. The first is called chawwára, a day-trip of 6 to 12 hours, inclusive of the time taken for cutting the reed. The cutting-down of a canoe-load, which is about 15 bundles of reed, takes about four hours. So, if the reed is near, the trip might take about six hours.

When it takes more than four hours to reach the reed, the reed gatherers spend a night on the spot. Those men who own large sailing-boats take their boats, together with their small canoes, on long reed-gathering expeditions, leaving their womenfolk behind. They spend about a month or so sleeping and preparing their food in the boats without putting up huts or shelters. The length of the expedition depends on the size of the sailing-boat.

Cutting down the reed is carried out with a wooden-handled, toothed sickle. The majority of reed cutters set out in pairs; one cuts and the other, usually a child or woman, performs the tasks of measuring, tying and loading.

Every villager has the full right to go anywhere in the Hor and cut reeds. But there are several rules observed among the cutters themselves. Firstly, a man (or group of men) entering a bed of reeds growing on both sides of a waterway will have the right to cut alone all that day without competition from anyone else. Secondly, during the jiniba season only, one group of reed-cutters, usually of the same family or lineage, can cut a circle round an area of reed, and thus acquire the right to cut all the reed in this area. Finally, reed-gathers should never take reeds cut and tied by somebody else. Owing to the extraordinary abundance of reed, none of these rules is broken nor in practice do any disputes arise from reed-cutting.

USE OF REEDS

Mat-weaving is the most important use for reeds. Huts and guest houses are built entirely from reeds and reed mats. Their earth floors are covered with mats. In each household one or two mats are kept handy to sit on while resting outside the hut. Mats are used during the agricultural season as covers for the crops and as stores or granaries both in the fields and in the huts. They are also used in making fences for the islands and for raising the floor of the island in the flood season.

More are used for making ṣobāt, which is a large platform from 11 to 19 feet in length, 11 to 14 feet in width and 6 to 9 feet in height, built to sleep on during the flood and hot season. In addition, reed is used in making a variety of furniture and home appliances such as beds, cots, baskets and canoe poles.

Of the two kinds of fuel used in ech-Chibayish, reed and cattle-dung, reed is the more widely used, as it is more plentiful.

Reeds are sold or bartered both inside and outside ech-Chibayish. In 1953 the current prices were:

	Uncut	Cut
100 bundles of ½ shrā'[1] in diameter	750 fils	500 fils
100 bundles of 1 shrā' in diameter	ID 1/500	ID 1/000
100 bundles of 2 shrā' in diameter	ID 3/000	ID 2/000

Outside ech-Chibayish the reed is taken to the three districts of il-Gharraf, il-Mijarra, and Amara. During the winter harvest season at least 200 families take reed to il-Gharraf. Some of it is split and beaten into plaited reed, and some is tied in bundles. There the plaited reeds are woven into mats and both reeds and mats are bartered for barley and wheat. Similarly, during the summer crop harvest at Amara and il-Mijarra, reeds and mats are bartered for rice and great millet. These journeys become more frequent in the years when no cultivation takes place at ech-Chibayish and those who do not cultivate go on them every year.

MAT-WEAVING TECHNIQUES

60 years ago the Beni Isad tribe lived by cultivation and cattle-keeping. They looked on mat-weaving with contempt, and only severe economic pressure (and even military coercion) forced them to take up the despised

---

[1] Shrā' is a native unit of length equivalent to about 18 inches—i.e. from the tip of the middle finger to the elbow.

occupation associated then with the Ma'dan inhabitants of th
They acquired the techniques only gradually and it is significa
change in the economy from cultivation to mat-weaving sta
periphery of the Beni Isad, those lineages and clans with ___ ___
standing being the last to take up the occupation. Before the beginning of
this century, some Ma'dan such as Albu Shbayib[1] and Il-Awachi,[2] who had
lived for a long time with Beni Isad and later became affiliated with them,
had already learnt to weave mats. Then some of Beni Isad who had originally been Ma'dan but were now affiliated with the tribe (such as segments
of il-Hadadiyīn and Ahl Wnais clans), learnt the art and also began to
weave. Towards the last days of Shaikh Hasan Ahl Khayūn (about 1890)
Beni Isad themselves began to learn. During the time of Shaikh Chayid
Ahl Khayūn (1893-1896), more and more of Beni Isad began to weave, as
cultivation became more unprofitable. During the war of 1914-1918, mat
prices were raised as there was a great demand from the British military
authorities who enforced supply. Under this simultaneous compulsion and
incentive, Beni Isad took up mat-weaving in earnest. The Ahl ish-Shaikh
clan was the slowest in taking up the new occupation and did not begin to
weave until after the 1914-1918 war. When the military demand ceased
Ahl ech-Chibayish had already learned the work and had found it profitable to export their mats. Certain lineages of Ahl ish-Shaikh, Ahl Anaisi,
Ahl Wais and Beni Aschiri clans did not learn to weave until as late as the
1930s. Those of Beni Isad who resisted this change of occupation supplemented their meagre incomes from cultivation by migratory labour. Later
they realized that even this did not ensure subsistence, and so began to take
to mat-weaving as their main occupation.

Ahl ech-Chibayish hate mat-weaving, though they are quite aware that
it is their principal source of income, since cultivation is hazardous and
unprofitable. They constantly complain that mat-weaving is a hard and
wearisome task, and that the most tiring part of it is the gathering and
transportation of reed from distant places. They even maintain that mat-
weaving causes leprosy, though there is no evidence for this. One of the
Ahl ech-Chibayish myths about mat-weaving is that *iblīs* (the Devil) began
weaving a mat, and he destroyed it, but *beni ādam* (man) found a part of it
and learnt the craft. That is why 'mat-weaving has no blessing and those
who practise it never make profit'.

Mats are woven on one common pattern and all the processes and techniques are uniform. But there is one lineage in the village, the Albu
Masāūd of the il-Hadadyīn clan, who are famed for their special skill in
this art. They specialize in weaving mats with woven edges and mats of
enormous size for huts and guest houses. There is always about ID 2/000
difference in price per thousand mats between those of Albu Mas'ūd and
those of other makes.

[1] Now a lineage of the Ahl ish-Shaikh clan of the Beni Isad tribe.
[2] A clan of Beni Isad living outside ech-Chibayish.

The time spent in producing mats depends largely on the time required
to reach the reed bed. Records of the different processes of skinning,
splitting, beating flat and weaving reed to make one mat, show that the
average time taken to complete a mat is about two hours. The average size
of the commercial mats woven at the village is about nine feet by five feet.

In a sample of 120 families, there were 75 (62·5 per cent) who practised
mat weaving; 27 of these families were solely dependent on mat-weaving
for their living, and the remaining 48 supplemented mat-weaving with
agriculture or other sources of income. In these 75 families, the average
daily output was 6·1 mats per family. In the 27 families who depended
entirely on mat-weaving, the average daily income was 47 *fils* per person.
The average daily income from mat-weaving in the other families not
entirely dependent on it was 30 *fils* per person.

MAT USE AND TRADE

During the year beginning 1 April 1952 Tariq Ahl Khayūn, the collector
of the municipal mat taxes, received ID 12,000 for 800,000 mats exported
from ech-Chibayish, on the basis of ID 1/500 per 100 mats. To estimate
the approximate number of mats produced at ech-Chibayish, the 800,000
exported has to be added to the number of mats used locally, which are
excluded from taxation, and the number of mats exported by private individuals and in small quantities without tax. There are about 2,000 huts
and about 600 guest houses in ech-Chibayish. Every hut needs roughly
15 mats per annum for covering and other domestic purposes. The
ordinary hut needs at least 25 mats when rebuilt every five years, so five
mats yearly per hut should be allowed. Further, every guest house needs
an average of 150 when rebuilt every 15 years. Thus it is reckoned that
about 40,000 mats are used for huts and 12,000 for guest houses every year,
while Tariq Ahl Khayūn himself has estimated that there are at least
10,000 mats exported without being taxed. The number of mats produced
at ech-Chibayish is thus approximately 862,000.

Three types of person are connected with the mat trade: the weaver,
the collector and the trader. The weavers, of whom there are about 1,000
families at ech-Chibayish, deal either through mat collectors, if they want
to sell their mats for money, or with the in-Nazil shops if they want to
barter them for goods. Each collector has about 30 families (called in this
context *maṣāni'*, lit. = factories). He acts as middle-man between them and
the trader who employs him. The family receives from the collector a sum
of money in advance, which is usually the equivalent of three or four days'
production by the family, and the collector comes daily in his canoe for the
mats produced. As both sides are illiterate, the collector keeps his accounts
in his head and refreshes his customers' memory every time he calls to
collect mats. Weavers have no relations whatever with the traders, except
through the collectors.

The mat collectors in ech-Chibayish number normally about 30, except during the seasonal boom when they are increased by about five, and at the slump when they are reduced to about 20. They work for the mat traders on a fixed commission-basis of ID 2/500 on every 1,000 mats collected. The collector receives daily a sum of money from the trader to distribute among the families weaving for him, and after collection the mats are put in stores owned by the trader. The collector is responsible for the mats till they are shipped. From time to time, especially at times of changing prices, the trader and the collector settle their accounts and the latter receives his commission.

Mat collectors are not necessarily related by kinship, lineage or clan affiliation to the families weaving for them, nor are they necessarily related to the mat traders. But in practice it is known that the work of a collector goes more smoothly when he is dealing with families of his own lineage or clan, and mat traders prefer such collectors. Secondly, both the traders and weavers prefer to deal with collectors of good reputation who are known for their honesty, and for this reason some families stick to one collector in whom they have confidence regardless of other considerations. Neighbourhood is a third principle of organization. As we have seen, the village is more than three miles in length and naturally a collector living at one end of it will prefer to deal with families who live nearby.

Whereas in the mat collector's work it is an advantage to have ties of kinship and neighbourhood with the weavers, so that they will co-operate more readily, the opposite is true for the traders. If they were to listen to the claims of needy kinsmen, allow delays in paying debts, or make favourable adjustments according to the seasonal changes in the value of the mats, they would have little prospect of making a profit. It is, therefore, significant and interesting to see that four of the nine mat traders of ech-Chibayish are *sāda* and control more than 80 per cent of the export of mats from ech-Chibayish. The fact that they are *sāda*, and are therefore not related to either the collectors or weavers by kinship or lineage ties gives them a great advantage in their business. As we shall see these four *sāda* traders make use of their high religious status to improve their trading position.

EXPORT OF MATS

The mat traders ship their mats to Basra or to Baghdad via il-Gurna, or up the Euphrates to other towns. There are four seasons in the mat trade, determined both by the state of transportation and the accessibility of reed at different stages of growth and quality. The boom season is in March, April, May and June, when water is high and communication up the river is open. Large barges towed by launches, sailing-boats and other vessels go daily from ech-Chibayish to a number of Euphrates towns as far as il-Fallūja. The greatest proportion of the output of ech-Chibayish mats is shipped during these four months, since this period of maximum shipping facilities coincides with the season of *jiniba*, which makes the most valuable mats.

July and the first half of August is a period of transition from the season of *jinība*, to that of the lower quality *'agga*. Both *'agga* and *jinība* mats have to be shipped down stream, mainly to Basra, as the end of the flood cuts communication up stream.

From the middle of August till November is the *'agga* season when mats fetch lower prices. At the same time communication up the river is still cut by low water, so all the mats go down river to Basra where they are needed in the date-packing stations. Some of the mats go to Baghdad via il-Gurna by the Tigris.

During the months of December, January and February there is a slump in the export trade. The river is navigable only by very small craft. At the same time, the demand for mats is small, because freight charges for the much heavier green reed mats of the current season are high in relation to the actual number of mats shipped, and so the margin of profit on the export is smaller. Mats are sent mostly to Basra, but one or two barges go to Baghdad via il-Gurna. During these three months traders restrict their activities and cut down the number of their collectors and consequently there is reduced pressure on the weavers. Many families take advantage of this and undertake expeditions to barter mats and reed for cereals with Amara and il-Mijarra. Traders stock small quantities of mats against the next boom season in March.

MAT BARTER

When mat debts accumulate, collectors threaten to stop giving substantial advances, or may even stop advances completely in cases of heavy debts. If they need money for daily necessities, or for clothing, canoe repairs and so on, the weavers may take their mats to sell or barter them, behind the collector's back, either in ech-Chibayish or outside it. They tell the mat collector that they have not been able to weave.

There are about 50 shops in the in-Nazil section of the village, which barter mats. The prices of goods sold at these shops are usually about 10 per cent higher than those in the village market, in which only cash transactions may be made. Since these shops buy mats for cash or exchange commodities for them, and because they are scattered evenly over the in-Nazil section, Ahl ech-Chibayish prefer to deal with them rather than with the market shops. Also the shopkeepers act as mat traders and leave the collector's commission of 250 *fils* per 100 mats to their customers as they need not employ collectors. This makes the prices ID 3/250 and ID 2/250 per 100 mats instead of ID 3/000 and ID 2/000. The families who are in debt to the collectors prefer to dispose of their mats by barter in these shops, appreciating the better prices they receive as weavers and not noticing the higher price they pay as customers. In fact the advantages obtained from the facilities of barter and the better prices for mats offered by these shops are offset by the fact that indebted families who barter their mats frequently there overlook their debts to the mat traders and consequently lose through the process of *galab*[1] more than they gain from trade with the in-Nazil shops.

The in-Nazil shops use the same system of seasonal changing of the prices and number of mats as the basis of calculation of loans, in their business transactions. The shopkeepers encourage their customers to buy more goods than they can afford, as they gain by drawing them into debt. If the indebted customers pay regularly, the shopkeepers gain stable supplies of mats, if not, the process of changing prices and the number of mats owed will greatly increase the shopkeeper's ultimate profit.

Such shops usually sell and barter sugar, tea, tobacco, cigarette paper, flour, boxes of matches and kerosene. The barter is always carried out in terms of money values. A man bringing ten mats, for example, will acquire the right to buy goods to the equivalent of the price of these ten mats, i.e. 300 *fils* if the mats are *jiniba*, and 200 *fils* if they are *'agga*. He might buy goods to the value of this money, spend part and receive the rest in cash, or deposit the whole sum with the shopkeeper.

I noticed that mat weavers attach much less value to mats than to their equivalent in money. They will cheerfully give ten mats for commodities in the shop, but on receiving 300 *fils* from the shopkeeper hesitate to spend it. Most shopkeepers are aware of this and do their utmost not to hand the weavers money. The most general plan seemed to be to keep the weavers always in debt by giving them a loan of goods in advance.

Outside the village, mats are bartered in three districts, usually during the months of December, January and February, when there is a lull in the shipping of mats. Mats are usually taken in small quantities to il-Mijarra in canoes, but if a larger vessel is available, they are taken either to Amara or il-Gharraf. They are normally bartered for cereals, especially rice. The prices of mats in Amara and il-Mijarra are about double the corresponding prices at ech-Chibayish and as cereals can be obtained at cheaper prices there than at ech-Chibayish, the gain from such barter is always considerable. At il-Gharraf conditions are even better, since reed is rare there, but the journey is long and rice is dearer than it is in the Amara or il-Mijarra districts.

I was not able to obtain any figures of people engaged in these barter expeditions, but estimate that 200 families at least send one of their members in a canoe, or more in a larger vessel, to one of these three districts every year. In many cases barter is carried out on the basis of one *wijiya* of rice for one mat. The *fellahin* of the district to which mats are taken to be bartered are prepared to pay only 60 *fils* for a mat but will barter it for one *wijiya* of rice (3·75 Kg.) which would actually fetch 80 *fils* in the market. The price of one *wijiya* of rice in ech-Chibayish market would be 120 *fils*, and in an in-Nazil shop it could be obtained for four mats. The ech-Chibayish mat-weavers thus make considerable profit in these exchanges.

[1] *galab*—a type of agreement by which the amount of a debt is increased if the debtor fails to repay it within the season.

The attraction of barter at these rates is so strong that in itself it directs a considerable proportion of the supply of mats away from the trader to whom the weaver is indebted. Consequently, it tends to increase barter with in-Nazil shops, delays the repayment of the trader's advances and thus automatically increases the weaver's indebtedness to him. This process, however, is limited by the close watch kept by mat collectors on families indebted to them. Moreover, it is not practicable for families in the hands of these collectors and traders to save mats or reed, because they would not receive money in advance unless they offered mats regularly. Thus, most of the people who go outside ech-Chibayish to barter their mats and reeds are in fact among those who are free from mat debts in the village.

II

Economic Balance

F ROM the foregoing chapters it is clear that this is not a subsistence economy, but one strongly specialized in mat-weaving for export, in which the people are dependent on imports for most of their food requirements and for all their clothing and other necessities. We have shown how mat-weaving is supplemented by uncertain and unprofitable summer cultivation, by labour migrations and expeditions, by cattle-rearing and by occasional fishing and fowling. But for the most part, production in ech-Chibayish means production of mats for export: there is practically no internal exchange of goods.

An assessment of the relative values of ech-Chibayish imports and exports presents great difficulties. There are no reliable official data and individuals are accustomed to conceal information on the extent of their enterprises. What I have already said about mat and cereal production will be enough to show the difficulties of making such an assessment.

TRADE AND MARKET

The external trade of ech-Chibayish comprises mats and cereals as exports, and food, clothes, tobacco and other commodities as imports. Internal distribution is carried out by the village market, the local cereal traders and millers and the Ma'dan women traders.

There are nine mat traders in ech-Chibayish: four of them control the trade of about 80 per cent of the exported mats. Together with the 35 shops at in-Nazil dealing with mats, they purchase and barter all the mats woven in ech-Chibayish and ship them to various parts of the country. They work through about 30 mat collectors and have certain collecting and shipping centres.

All the cereal produce of the region is sent to Basra. There are six traders in ech-Chibayish from two *sāda* families, who compete with one another for the cereal trade in years when cultivation has taken place. Between them they buy not only the crop sold in ech-Chibayish, but that of other nearby marsh villages and communities. They ship the crop either on their own account or for one of the big trading firms at Basra from whom they receive substantial commission. It was not possible to estimate the profit made by these exporters, because the two families concerned also run shops and mat-trading centres, and ship both cereals and mats

for themselves and for other traders. Trade or shipment of different commodities are not itemized in their trading accounts so that an estimate of
a single item is in practice impossible. The six traders buy most of the crop
before it is ripe, or even before it is actually planted, on the *akhaḍar*
system.[1] Moreover, they purchase all the crop offered for sale directly
from the fields immediately after it is divided. They have collecting agents
to whom they give a percentage of the profit.

The export of cereals is important only in years of cultivation when the
usual import of cereal food is much reduced, the traders reserving for local
sale as much as they consider can be absorbed by the local market. Normally, however, cereals are imported in considerable quantities from
Basra either as flour or grain. There are five shopkeepers who specialize
entirely in the import and sale of cereals. Their monthly profits range
between ID 10/000 and ID 20/000.

Other imports are sugar, tea, tobacco and cloth, bought in large quantities by the individual shopkeepers, together with the other commodities
less in demand. The only two centres with which ech-Chibayish shopkeepers deal are il-Gurna and Basra. As il-Gurna prices are higher than
those of Basra, most of the ech-Chibayish shopkeepers prefer to make the
longer trip to Basra. There they buy from wholesale traders and ship their
purchases by sailing boat or motor launch and sometimes by motor lorry
to il-Gurna. From il-Gurna there is a regular daily motor launch service
to ech-Chibayish by which commodities are usually shipped. During
high water, shipment can be arranged from Basra to ech-Chibayish
directly by boat.

Ech-Chibayish market is composed of two groups of shops: in-Nahiya
and in-Nazil. There are 65 in-Nahiya shops, built of bricks with mat
and log roofs. As they are usually called *is-sūg* (the market), I shall call
them the market shops, to distinguish them from the island shops. They
are usually 9 by 15 feet in size, and stand in line along the river front. In
contrast, the 35 in-Nazil shops are scattered among the dwelling islands.
They are indistinguishable from ordinary reed dwelling huts, except for
distinctive little white flags.

Conditions of business in the two groups of shops are quite different.
While the market shops sell for cash only, the island reed shops mostly
barter for mats as well as selling for cash. There is a noticeable difference
in the class of commodities sold in the two kinds of shops. While in the
market shops there are many varieties of foodstuffs, cloth, domestic
utensils, and luxuries, the island shops sell only flour, sugar, tea, tobacco,
matches, kerosene and cloth. Although the island shops sell what are regarded as bare necessities, their prices are about ten per cent higher than
in the market shops. In spite of the smaller variety of goods they offer and
their smaller turnover, the island shops succeed in drawing considerable
custom from the market shops. In fact, some of the island shopkeepers

[1] See p. 131.

have been known to make fortunes and many are richer than the shop-keepers of the market. The main profits come from the sale of mats. Were the market shopkeepers prepared to accept payment in mats, it is almost certain that they would put their island rivals out of business. Transport and storage difficulties alone do not account for their refusal to adopt the most profitable business methods. Considerations of prestige operate here to the detriment of professional interests, even among those who have to a large extent abandoned the values of tribal life. These shopkeepers pride themselves on having adopted the values of townspeople, civilized stan-dards of conduct, including cash business instead of the obviously pro-fitable mat-barter which they despise as an uncivilized method of trading.

54 shop premises in in-Nahiya were owned by nine people, individually or in partnership. 45 shops only were occupied, and the remainder had been vacant for some time. Of the 45 in business, 32 were occupied by tenants and 13 by their owners. The monthly rents of the shops, differing according to the size of the shop and its location in the market, varied from ID 2/000 to ID 0/400.

Of the 45 occupied shops there were 16 grocers, 13 cloth merchants—3 of whom did tailoring as well as selling cloth—5 tailors, 2 flour sellers, 4 coffee shops, 1 barber, 1 dyer, 1 ironmonger, 2 haberdashers. Monthly earnings were estimated through direct investigation, and information secured from the market shopkeepers themselves has a fair degree of accuracy. 1 shop earned more than ID 30/000, 4 about 20/000, 12 between ID 10 and 20/000. 15 little shops earned less than ID 5/000 a month.

THE ISLAND SHOPS

In 1953 there were 35 island shops. About 20 were big permanent shops all of which bartered and sold sugar, tea, tobacco, cloth, flour and kerosene, and other popular commodities. The remaining 15 were small shops which did not deal in flour or cloth, but bartered, or sometimes sold, small quantities of sugar, tea, tobacco and boxes of matches.

All these shops were built on the shopkeepers' own dwelling islands. Some of them were run in dwelling huts and were by no means permanent. Their monthly profits varied between ID 30/000 and ID 3/000. Six shops made a profit of over ID 20/000, and seven made under ID 4/000.

In addition to the shops, there are two flour mills in in-Nazil. Both mills charge one *fil* for grinding a kilogramme of cereal. The two owners of the first mill are landholders, and the owner of the second is an *akhaḍar* trader. All three, therefore, have crop shares when there is cultivation, and act as cereal traders. They buy great millet and wheat from tradesmen in ech-Chibayish, grind it in their mills and sell it both in their own shops and to the village shops.

The last important agents of distribution in the village are Ma'dan women traders. The majority are from il-Amaira and il-Fartūs tribes and they come daily. two in a canoe, from places between two and four hours' paddling distance from ech-Chibayish. They usually arrive in the morning and start back home early in the afternoon. They sell fish, game, milk, whey, curds, cheese, clarified butter, dung discs, and during the high-water season, when the surface of every island needs to be raised, they sell reeds and earth as well. As earth fetches high prices at these times, the Ma'dan search the Hor for the little uninhabited islands and ridges which are not covered by water and dig earth from them. During May they sell a sweet-meat made from a powder collected from the upper tips of bulrushes. They paddle through in-Nazil, calling out their wares, and the inhabitants summon them to stop to sell on the banks of the islands. As the Ma'dan women use unstandardized stones and bricks as weights, and as demand always exceeds supply, haggling and quarrels are the distinctive features of this trade. Most of these women traders do not go as far as the market section of the village, fearing both the lawful and unlawful taxes and dues imposed on them. Those who do go to the village market deal with the shops, selling them clarified butter or cheese, or they may sit in the market selling curds, whey, cheese, fish, game and dung. Usually each group deals with a certain shop, supplies it regularly with cheese and clarified butter and buys from it sugar, tea and tobacco. During 1953, the current price of clarified butter at ech-Chabiyish was ID 1/200 per *wijia*, which the shopkeepers buy from Ma'dan women traders at 900 *fils*, making a profit of 300 *fils* per *wijia*. From the islands, Ma'dan women traders buy eggs which they collect and take to wholesale traders at Basra. Eggs are bought for five *fils* per egg and together with the great millet can sometimes be bartered for fish, dairy produce and any other commodities the Ma'dan women sell.

There are two women of ech-Chibayish who practise a limited trade in the village. One sells bread at the market and the other runs a canoe-shop, selling cosmetics. Normally ech-Chibayish despise this way of earning a living, but both of these women have excuses for their deviation from tradition.

ECONOMIC STRATIFICATION

The unequal distribution of resources among the population produces six distinct economic classes; rich men, landholders, shopkeepers, artisans, employees, mat-weavers and cultivators.

The people recognize these classes and speak of them as if they were quite distinct groups, defined only by relative control of resources and standards of living. In practice the distinctions made on occupational criteria do not always correlate exactly with economic advantages. While undoubtedly the 'rich men' are the richest, and the landholders come next to them in wealth, the third class, that of the shopkeepers, contains some very wealthy men who may even rival the 'rich men' and also many whose economic standing is more comparable to that of artisans and employees. Again, the artisans are classed as being above the employees, although their income is about the same, because their occupation carries greater prestige.

I include this distinction, which is not based on income, in the description of economic classes because this is how Ahl ech-Chibayish think of it.

'RICH MEN'

About 20 persons representing 15 families occupied in the mat and cereal trade or deriving incomes from shopkeeping, moneylending, land mortgage, running motor launches, and the ownership of shops and houses, are called 'rich men'.

The actual capital in the hands of a rich man at any particular time is, in practice, difficult to conceal. Most of it is in the form of cash which is kept in iron safes in their shops or houses. Capital assets, such as motor launches, shop buildings, land mortgages, etc., can easily be assessed at their market values. Attempts at assessing the extent of one another's business is a regular subject of conversation in the market, and I found that there was remarkably little divergence between the various estimates made. In many cases I was able to verify these popular estimates by consulting the persons concerned and found that they readily conceded the accuracy of public opinion about the value of their property. The six richest men I could not approach with direct questions, but my own estimate of the value of their visible property and of their business went far to confirm the reliability of the general opinion in the market.

The four richest, engaged in cereal and mat-trading, money lending and land mortgage, were estimated to have capital worth ID 30,000. The four next richest, in the same occupations, were reliably placed in the ID 20,000 bracket. The six richest of these eight were members of the Bait Sayyid Khalaf lineage. The ninth had an estimated capital of ID 10,000. The 11 remaining members of this class varied betweed ID 5,000 and ID 1,000.

It is not possible to make an approximate estimate of the monthly profit of the eight richest men as their range of business is wide and fluctuates according to the seasons. But certainly the net mean monthly profit of each member is no less than ID 100/000. Hasan Ahl Bander, Haji Abid Ahl Mishad, Nasir Ahl Rahag and Sayyid Baqir is-Sayyid Ali, were each estimated to earn about ID 50/000 per month. The remaining eight persons earn between ID 20/000 and ID 30/000 per month.

LANDHOLDERS

About 20 men, including the *şirkals* of the clans, constitute the landholders. Agricultural land cannot be sold, it can only be mortgaged. The economic advantage enjoyed by this class is that, as landholders, they have the *fellahin* to cultivate their lands and with the proceeds of the sale of cereals they can maintain a higher standard of living than that of the cultivators and mat-weavers. They can keep guest houses, eat better food and live in better homes. They gain their income without manual labour and at the same time enjoy the prestige conferred on them by the holding of land. But those who, as *şirkals* of large clans, have heavy social obligations, cannot rely on the income from the land they hold to cover their expenses and have to supplement it. Some do this by making levies on their clansmen, others by cultivating patches of land for themselves, and one gets help from his sons who have gone into business. On the whole, members of this class enjoy what is regarded as a comfortable standard of living, but in terms of money income and capital they are not rich men and cannot accumulate property.

SHOPKEEPERS

About 70 men are involved permanently in shopkeeping as a full-time job. Their profits have already been discussed and compared.

THE ARTISANS

There are 11 full-time canoe builders and repairers scattered over the village. Their estimated monthly incomes range from ID 9/000 to ID 3/000. The majority repair and caulk canoes, but they rarely build new ones: in fact, only three of them are capable of building a canoe. The raw materials for both building and repairs—planks (for which the inferior wood from the packing cases of imported commodities is usually used), nails, bitumen, reeds as fuel for the furnace, and crude oil—are supplied by the owner of the canoe.

Canoe builders and repairers work on their islands and are usually helped both by younger members of their families and by the owner of the canoe. Each has an earthen furnace to melt bitumen for caulking.

There are five artisans who specialize in hut and guest house building at ech-Chibayish. For guest houses they are paid between ID 10/000 and ID 20/000 and some clothes or cereal, according to the size of the guest house built and the length of time taken over the work. When the guest house of the Ahl ish-Shaikh ṣirkal, Abdil-Hadi Ahl Khayūn, was built in February and March 1953, the artisan Mizhir Ahl Nashtar was given at the end of 28 days' work, ID 10/000 and an outer cloak worth ID 3/000. The building of guest houses is not frequent. During my stay at ech-Chibayish four guest houses were built and one was repaired. It can, therefore, provide only a limited source of income to the five artisans. None of them relies upon this craft as his main job; they weave mats and cultivate as others do. They are not given wages for building the usual dwelling huts, as any members of the lineage concerned may be called to assist.

The blacksmiths of ech-Chibayish are all Ṣubba (Mandaeans). There were only three families of Mandaeans at ech-Chibayish during 1953, two of which lived and worked together. They live by blacksmithing alone, and make fishing spears, reed splitters, sickles, and nails for the canoes and larger boats. The iron used is bought from Basra and the fuel burned is locally extracted from reeds by the blacksmiths themselves in kilns specially built for this purpose. The average monthly income of each family appeared to be between ID 6/000 and ID 9/000 and there is a greater demand for their tools during winter than during summer.

The only five cloth-weavers at ech-Chibayish are of one lineage, Ahl Hlal of Ahl Ghrīj clan. Though there is a great demand for a coarse plain woollen cloth used as outer cloaks by men and women, it is not generally woven at the village except by these five weavers, and the excess demand has to be met by imports. This craft is utterly despised by the other clans and lineages, and, as a consequence, is dying out. Four of the five weavers do not work for more than seven months a year as they join the migrations to the il-Gharraf region and to the date-packing stations; whilst the remaining one works nine months, and migrates to il-Gharraf region for three months every year. The loom used is an extremely crude type of 'frame-heald' loom, built of wood and reed. The weaver works sitting on the ground in the open air, working the healds with his feet from a pit. He is prevented from working for the three or four months of flood, because this pit is then filled with water. The average prices paid for weaving a piece of cloth sufficient to make a cloak, which takes about four days, is about 200 *fils*. Prices vary according to the texture of the cloth required. Because of the irregularity of their work it was impossible to estimate the weavers' average income.

EMPLOYEES

19 men are employed at the government offices and the native mills as policemen, messengers, caretakers, labourers and clerks. Their salaries range from ID 3/000 to ID 8/000 per month.

The three policemen supplement their incomes by bribes, amounting to an average of ID 5/000 monthly. The municipal workers have no other source of income, but the five office messengers receive small gifts from people who call at the offices and one of them receives financial assistance from his two sons, who work outside ech-Chibayish. The two school caretakers each earn about ID 3/000 per month for nine months for providing meals for the non-native teachers whose families are not with them, and they do a limited amount of trade selling vegetables during the remaining three months of the summer vacation.

MAT-WEAVERS AND CULTIVATORS

The five previous classes were composed of about 145 families, i.e. nine per cent of the 1,604 families of ech-Chibayish. The remaining 91 per cent are mat-weavers, cultivators and labour migrants; and the great majority depend wholly on mat-weaving as the main source of livelihood. I have estimated that the average daily income of a family of this class composed of four persons (a husband, wife, boy and girl) is about 150 *fils*, making the monthly average income ID 4/500.

STANDARD OF LIVING

The classification given above of six economic classes recognized by the people of ech-Chibayish is in part a classification according to occupational

I

status, and does not correspond completely to important differences in the standard of living of these groups.

The mat-weavers and cultivators barely meet their needs. The minimum standard of living for a family at ech-Chibayish is as follows: food—great millet, bread and tea sufficient for the three meals of the day, with an occasional evening meal of boiled rice, and midday meal of fish; tobacco—for the men only; clothes—one robe for each member of the family, replaced only when it is completely worn out.

A large number of mat-weavers and cultivators cannot earn enough to enjoy even this standard without incurring debts. Those who own a few head of cattle and who can therefore supplement their diet with dairy products are in a better position than the others; and the few who can keep themselves clear of debt are again in a relatively advantageous position.

Going up the scale from the mat-weavers to the employees and artisans, we find very little difference in the standard of living but the fixed salary of the employees provides some security for them; and since the work of the artisans is paid on a scale much higher than anything that can be earned by a weaver, they can be expected to pay off any debts they may incur.

But the shopkeepers, landholders and the rich men do enjoy higher standards. Most of them live in larger huts and about ten of the wealthy families live in brick houses which provide additional comfort, security from flooding, and healthier conditions. In their homes furniture and utensils are of better quality and they own bedsteads, clothes chests and carpets. Men and women of this class usually have surplus clothes and nearly all their boys go to the village school. They enjoy a more varied and nutritious diet, usually consisting of wheat-bread, rice, fish, curds, whey, game and, occasionally, meat. These three top classes have a common standard of living, despite differences in the amount of property they own. This is not because the rich men and wealthy landholders and shopkeepers do not appreciate higher standards. Many have modern furniture and a few use hurricane lamps and buy ice during the very hot days of summer. Some of them even have wireless sets. But it seems that what prevents most of them from using their property to achieve a better standard of living is that the accumulation of wealth is regarded as an end in itself.

MAT-WEAVERS' GENERAL ECONOMIC PATTERN

All mat-weavers practise weaving during the year till the agricultural season arrives. If there is to be cultivation, those who cultivate abandon mat-weaving for one month to concentrate on agricultural activities. At times of migrations and expeditions, those who participate in such economic activities, leave the village for the periods of labour.

Each family tends to deal with one shop from which it gets sugar, tea, tobacco, flour and cloth. Most of the buying is done on credit, as cash plays but a small part in such transactions. The head of the family hands

over all the cash income or all the mats woven to the shopkeeper who
supplies him with the family necessities, keeping a written account. From
time to time the head of the family is notified by the shopkeeper of the
amount of debt, and if debts are accumulating and no payment is being
made, the shopkeeper ceases to supply the family.

For buying bigger items, such as a robe or a head cloth, and for paying
larger sums of money, such as a brideprice, a share of compensation, etc.,
they sell a calf or a cow, or raise loans, either from the shopkeepers or from
the moneylenders, though a few families may be fortunate enough to have
a profit available from occasional cultivation.

The average monthly cost of food for a family of mat-weavers composed,
say, of the two parents, a boy, a girl, and an infant, enjoying a medium
standard of living, is estimated as follows:

Item of food	Cost (ID) per month
6 *wijia* flour (great millet)	0/420
6 *wijia* flour (mixed wheat)	0/720
4 *wijia* rice	0/640
Sugar and tea	1/500
ghumūs, i.e. any food which supplements the staple bread and boiled rice, such as fish and dairy products	1/000
Tobacco (for men only)	0/600
	4/880

These estimates are based on the current village prices during 1953, and
are made on the assumption that all the food is imported, as is the case in
years when agriculture is impossible. It may be reckoned that an adult
male, buying all his food from the village market, will need for food per
month:

Item of food	Cost (fils) per month
2 *wijia* of flour (great millet)	140
2 *wijia* of flour (mixed wheat)	240
1 *wijia* of rice	160
Sugar and tea	550
ghumūs	375
Tobacco	600
	ID 2/065

Few men do not smoke, and only a very small number of women do smoke.
The average monthly cost for food, excluding the cost of tobacco, is then
ID 1/465. A boy or girl between 6 and 14 years of age is estimated as con-
suming food worth ID 1/000 per month, and a child between two and five
years of age is estimated as costing ID 0/600.

The cost of clothes is as follows:

FOR A MAN

Articles of clothing	Annual average cost (ID)
2 summer robes (*dishdāsha*). (Each needs to be replaced about every three months)	1/400
1 winter robe (of stronger material and less frequently washed, lasts all the cold season)	0/900
2 headkerchiefs (*chafiya*)	0/700
2 outer cloaks (*bishit*), a summer one which costs ID 1/500, and a winter one costing ID 2/250, lasting together four years	1/000
1 jacket costs ID 1/000 and lasts two years	0/500
1 head rope (*'agāl*) costs 500 *fils* and lasts three years	0/167
2 pairs of trunks	0/400
1 pair of slippers (*na'āl*)	0/200
	ID 5/267
Average monthly cost	ID 0/439

FOR A WOMAN

Article of clothing	Average annual cost (ID)
2 summer robes	1/400
1 winter robe	1/000
2 summer head cloths *shela*	0/400
1 winter head cloth	0/250
1 head band *chafiya*	0/200
1 outer cloak costs ID 1/000 and lasts two years	0/500
	ID 3/750
Average monthly cost	ID 0/312

FOR A BOY

Article of clothing	Average annual cost (ID)
2 summer robes	1/000
1 winter robe	0/600
1 headkerchief	0/300
1 pair of trunks	0/150
1 jacket costs ID 0/500 for every two years	0/250
	ID 2/300
Average monthly cost	ID 0/191

FOR A GIRL

Article of clothing	Average annual cost (ID)
2 summer robes	0/700
1 winter robe	0/500
2 head cloths	0/200
	ID 1/400
Average monthly cost	ID 0/117

FOR AN INFANT

Article of clothing	Average annual cost (ID)
3 robes, two for summer and one for winter	0/450
	ID 0/450
Average monthly cost	ID 0/037

According to these estimates the monthly expenditure of such a family may be estimated as follows:

Estimated Monthly Expenditure of a Man, a Woman, a Boy, a Girl, and an Infant of the Mat-Weavers' and Cultivators' Class

	Food (ID)	Clothing (ID)	Total (ID)
Man	2/065	0/439	2/504
Woman	1/465	0/312	1/777
Boy	1/000	0/191	1/191
Girl	1/000	0/117	1/117
Infant	0/600	0/037	0/637
Total	6/130	1/096	7/226

Average monthly earning of a family of four is ID 4/500.

The following are detailed budgets of five families, selected from five different clans of the tribe, and of different composition ranging from five to ten persons. The ways in which their various members earned their living embraced all the possibilities open to the mat-weavers and cultivators.

These budgets were gathered over a period of six months only (July to December 1953). It was not possible to extend the period over the whole year which I spent at the village because it was not desirable to carry out such investigations during the first six months of my residence among Ahl ech-Chibayish when they lacked confidence in me, and my knowledge of their society was inadequate. However, in the mat-weavers' and cultivators' economy, there is very little difference in the income of the various months of the year, and thus no serious errors need be made in working out budgets based on data gathered over six months only. The slump in mat production during the 'agga and jiniba seasons is compensated by the fluctuation in the prices of mats. Similarly, debt evens out expenditure since families have to hand over all their incomes and are given cash and commodities enough only for their bare necessities.

There is the usual difficulty of assessing the incomes of people who rely partly on their cash earnings and partly on their own subsistence output.[1] However, as ech-Chibayish is not a subsistence economy and as everything which is consumed and produced can be used in exchange, it is not difficult to give a cash value to those commodities which are consumed directly by the producers: milk and dairy products where a cow is owned, dates where date palms are owned, and grain in the cases where cultivation has been carried out.

HOUSEHOLD I

Thamir Ahl Abdalla's family (Ahl Ghrij clan)

Composition of household: 3 men, 3 women, 1 boy, 1 girl, 1 infant.
Resources: Cultivation. Fishing expedition. Date-packing and il-Gharraf migrations. 26 date palms.

	Monthly average income (ID)
(a) *Cultivation*	
Net family share of crop (great millet) = 15 *mann* of ID 1/800 'on farm' prices, total = ID 27/000	2/250
2 *mann* consumed by the family during one month on the farm, price = ID 3/600	0/300
(b) *Fishing expedition*	
2 male members participated and earned ID 7/000 each, total = ID 14/000	1/166
(c) *Date-packing migration*	
1 woman and 1 man migrated to Basra and earned ID 20/000 net. While there they spent ID 6/000 during 2 months, total = ID 26/000	2/166
(d) *il-Gharraf migration*	
No profit. 8 members composed of 5 adults and 3 children migrated for three months and earned only what they consumed. Estimated cost of living during migration 325 *fils* per day, ID 29/250 for the three months	2/437
(e) *Date palms*	
The family owns 26 palms, 23 of which are female palms. The output of each (consumption, sale and fuel) was estimated as 400 *fils* per annum, and 3 male palms the return of each (fuel only) is 50 *fils*, total = ID 9/350	0/779
Total family net monthly income	ID 9/098

[1] Professor Daryll Forde in his *The Native Economies of Nigeria* (London, 1950, pp. 35–9) and Phyllis Deane in her book *The Measurement of Colonial National Incomes* (Cambridge, 1948, pp. 19–20) have discussed this problem.

I was not able to obtain comparable figures for the actual expenditure of this family, or of any of the five families. It would have been too difficult to arrive at any clear estimate of the prices paid for the actual commodities acquired, since these prices varied according to the method of acquisition—barter or cash—the place of purchase, and since every purchase involved calculations of debt and interest between the parties. I was only able to compare income with expenditure on the basis of the average monthly expenditure calculated above. The estimated monthly expenditure of this family according to the table on p.123 would be:

	Food (ID)	Clothing (ID)	Total (ID)
3 men	6/195	1/317	7/512
3 women	4/395	0/936	0/331
1 boy	1/000	0/191	1/191
1 girl	1/000	0/117	1/117.
2 children	1/200	0/074	1/274
			ID 16/425

Total family monthly deficit   ID   7/327

Debts: The family has had debts amounting to about ID 300/000 for more than three years.

<h3 style="text-align:center">HOUSEHOLD II</h3>

Hsain Ahl Abba's family (Ahl Khatir clan)

Composition of household: 1 man artisan, 4 women.
Resources: Mat-weaving. Canoe repairs. 19 date palms. 6 cows.

	Monthly average income (ID)
(a) *Mat-weaving*	
Reeds gathered daily = 10 bundles, mats woven = 5, price = 150 *fils* for 5 mats	4/500
(b) *Canoe repairs*	
Average 10 canoes are repaired per month, average wages 150 *fils* for each	1/500
(c) *Date palms*	
18 female and 1 male palm, average total output per annum = ID 7/250	0/604
(d) *Cows*	
6 cows, each gives one calf per annum, valued at ID 3/000 and ID 3/600 worth of dairy produce per annum, total = ID 39/600	3/300
	ID 9/904

The estimated monthly expenditure of this family would be:

	Food (ID)	Clothing (ID)	Total (ID)
1 man	2/065	0/439	2/504
4 women	5/860	1/248	7/108

ID 9/712

Total family monthly profit   ID 0/192

HOUSEHOLD III
Jabir Ahl Mtashar's family (Ahl Anaisi clan)

Composition of household: 3 men, 1 woman, 2 children.
Resources: Mat-weaving. Cultivation. Il-Gharraf migration. 15 date palms.

Monthly average income (ID)

(a) Mat-weaving
Reeds gathered = 12 bundles per day, mats woven
= 6, price = 180 *fils* per day   5/400

(b) Cultivation
Net family share of crop (great millet) = 17 *mann*,
price 'on farm' = ID 30/600   2/550
1 *mann* was consumed by the family during one
month on the farm, price ID 1/800   0/150

(c) Il-Gharraf migration
The net profit of the family was ID 6/000. During
the migration the family consumed the value of
ID 22/500 (4 adults = 200 *fils* and 2 children =
50 *fils*, total = 250 per day). Total earning from
migration = ID 28/500   2/375

(d) Date palms
15 female palms, total annual output = ID 6/000   0/500

ID 10/975

From the total annual income of the family, the income of four months'
mat-weaving which was suspended during the three months of il-Gharraf
migration, and one month during cultivation, must be deducted. That
equals ID 21/600 which is ID 1/800 per month.

ID 10/975
ID 1/800

Total family net monthly income   ID 9/175

The estimated monthly expenditure of this family would be:

	Food (ID)	Clothing (ID)	Total (ID)
3 men	6/195	1/317	7/512
1 woman	1/465	0/312	1/777
2 children	1/200	0/074	1/274

ID 10/563

Total family monthly deficit   ID 1/388

Debts: The family is in debt to the amount of ID 25/000.

HOUSEHOLD IV
Khdhayir Ahl Flayih's family (Ahl Wais clan)

Composition of household: 1 man, 2 women, 3 children.
Resources: Mat-weaving. Cultivation. Il-Gharraf migration. 5 date palms.

Monthly average income (ID)

(a) *Mat-weaving*
Reeds gathered per day = 8 bundles which make
    4 mats, price = 120 *fils*   3/600

(b) *Cultivation*
Net family share of crop (great millet) = 7 *mann*,
    price 'on farm' = ID 12/600   1/050
About one *mann* was consumed by the family on
    the farm during one month, price = ID 1/800   0/150

(c) *Il-Gharraf migration*
The net profit of the family was ID 5/000 during
    three months' migration. The family consumed
    about 250 *fils* per day which makes ID 22/500.
    The total profit = ID 27/500   2/290

(d) *Date palms*
The annual output of 5 female date palms =
    ID 2/000   0/166

ID 7/256

The income from four months' mat-weaving, which was suspended during the three months' migration to il-Gharraf and for one month during the agricultural season, must be subtracted from the total annual income of the family. That makes ID 14/400 which is ID 1/200 per month:

ID 7/256
ID 1/200

Total family net monthly income   ID 6/056

The estimated monthly expenditure of this family is:

	Food (ID)	Clothing (ID)	Total (ID)
1 man	2/065	0/439	2/504
2 women	2/930	0/624	3/554
3 children	1/800	0/111	1/911
			ID 7/969

Total family monthly deficit: ID 1/913

Debts: The family is in debt for ID 6/000.

HOUSEHOLD V
Hyal Ahl Hsain's family (Ahl ish-Shaikh clan)

Composition of household: 2 men, 3 women, 1 boy.

Resources: Mat-weaving. Cultivation. Outside financial assistance. 12 date palms. 4 cows.

	Monthly average income (ID)
(a) Mat-weaving	
Reeds gathered, 12-13 bundles per day, which make 6·5 mats, price = 195 *fils*	5/850
(b) Cultivation	
Net family share of crop = 3·5 *mann* rice, price = ID 7/000, and 9 *mann* great millet, price = ID 16/200. Total = ID 23/000	1/933
1½ *mann* was consumed by the family during one month on the farm (½ *mann* rice and 1 *mann* great millet), price = ID 2/800	0/233
(c) Outside financial assistance	
Hyal Ahl Hsain receives a monthly contribution of ID 5/000 from his brother who works outside ech-Chibayish	5/000
(d) Date palms	
11 female palms yield ID 4/400 and one male date palm yields 50 *fils*, total ID 4/450	0/371
(e) Cows	
4 cows, each gives a return of ID 6/600, total = ID 26/400	2/200
	ID 15/587

Mat-weaving was suspended during the agricultural season for one month. The sum of ID 5/850 must be deducted from the annual income, making ID 0/487 per month.

ID 15/587
ID 0/487
———
ID 15/100
———

Total family net monthly income   ID 15/100

The estimated monthly expenditure of this family is:

	Food (ID)	Clothing (ID)	Total (ID)
2 men	4/130	0/878	5/008
3 women	4/395	0/936	5/331
1 boy	1/000	0/191	1/191
			———
			ID 11/530

Total estimated family monthly surplus   ID 3/570

GENERAL COMMENTS ON INFORMATION YIELDED FROM FAMILY BUDGETS

Household I

The family has a large debt of some duration and has a current high deficit; they have no hope of paying off the debt. They survive and continue, despite the current deficit, because of the labour migrations and expeditions in which they participate, when they receive advances from labour contractors. This debt is an extreme case, even for Ahl Ghrīj, who have the highest rate of indebtedness in the village. As is the case with all Ahl Ghrīj clan, there is no mat-weaving which supplies regular income; in its place is the life of labour migrations and expeditions.

Households II and V

Both these households have a profit and are clear of debt. The reasons are:

(a) There is an artisan's monthly income in the case of household II and a monthly contribution from outside of ID 5/000 in household V.

(b) Both households have a number of cows; six in the case of household II and four in the case of household V.

(c) The human composition of both families is another important factor which entails more production. Household II is composed of five adults only, the artisan and four women who are highly important in mat production. Household V is composed of two men, three women and only one boy, who is not dependent, but a productive person in mat-weaving as he takes part regularly in reed-cutting and other mat-weaving processes.

Households III and IV

These two households represent the usual pattern of households among the lower economic class in having a small monthly deficit. It is important to notice that both households are composed of the same number of persons and follow the same occupations: mat-weaving, cultivation, labour migration to il-Gharraf. But while household III has a deficit of ID 1/388 and a debt of ID 25/000, household IV has a deficit of ID 1/913 and a debt of ID 6/000. The deficit in both cases can be attributed to the number of children in the household. Another reason is the absence of any cattle in household IV.

CREDIT AND INDEBTEDNESS

A large number of the mat-weavers and cultivators, though living at the lowest local standard, are chronically in debt. To remain solvent, feed and clothe one's family, and contribute to social obligations arising out of clan and lineage membership, is naturally every man's ideal. Failure to do so without borrowing may detract from a man's good reputation, but heavy indebtedness does not disqualify him from being regarded as one of the 'good fellows'. However, there is always the danger that if debts continue to accumulate without any prospect of redemption, the creditor may refuse to extend credit.

To prevent this, a kind of debt rotation, called 'putting one person's cap on another person's head', is resorted to. Debtors incur new debts to pay back their old creditors, thus becoming debtors to new creditors. Debtors are in the habit of taking slightly higher loans than the debts they wish to repay, to meet other urgent needs which have been postponed. So every debt transfer increases the scale of indebtedness. On the other hand, debt rotation encourages loans: it is favoured as a way of paying back old debts, it 'keeps the name' of the debtor and confers on him the prestige of being a 'good fellow' and a man who 'does not eat the property of others'. It is highly important to be, or at least to appear to be, a debtor who tries to repay his debts in due course, because, once a man is known to be the 'eater of others' property', he may not be able to raise further loans.

One effect of the custom of debt rotation is to distribute risks evenly between the moneylenders. 'A' runs up an account at shop No. 1, until his debt with the shopkeeper reaches proportions with which he cannot himself cope and which the shopkeeper is not likely to allow him to exceed. He goes to shop No. 2 and borrows a sum sufficient to pay off completely shopkeeper No. 1 and he starts the process again. The shopkeepers regard the giving of loans with practically no security as a means of competing for custom. This system, of course, operates only for small loans in the case of families such as those described in the family budgets of households III and IV, where earning capacity is regularly just slightly below expenditure.

There are four types of loans:

(a) *Bowari* (mats). Mat traders give as advances, through mat collectors, loans repayable by mats.

(b) *Naqid* (cash). Many shopkeepers and rich men give loans between ID 10/000 and ID 20/000 at interest ranging between 10 and 50 per cent per annum. In such cases promissory notes are taken and interest is deducted in advance from the money lent.

(c) *Business loans*. Of these there are two kinds. With the first the creditor becomes a shareholder of the business, taking half the profit and bearing half the losses. In the second, he charges the debtor one-third of the profit but does not share any loss.

(d) *Akhaḍar*.[1] This is the most widespread type of loan and is the predominant factor reducing the *fellah's* share of the crops. When cultivation is expected and the *fellahin* begin to think of getting money for the seedlings, all moneylenders cease to give any loans except on the *akhaḍar* system. In general the greatest proportion of *akhaḍar* loans are taken from the six grain traders of the two families of 'holy men', the Bait Sayyid Khalaf.

To obtain an *akhaḍar* loan, the *fellah* promises to sell a number of *manns* of the crop he intends to raise, before he buys the seedlings required. The moneylender buys the promised *mann* for between 800 *fils* and ID 1/000, which is about 44-50 per cent of its price 'on farm'. Sometimes this price is beaten down as low as 33 per cent if the crop is doubtful or if the *fellah* is not known to be trustworthy. The *mann* purchased in advance should be handed over on the field immediately after the crop division. So, the moneylender pays ID 9/000 for 10 *manns* which could fetch ID 18/000 valued at 'farm' prices, and which might fetch as much as ID 20/000 six months later, and ID 25/000 towards the next season. The profit of the moneylender is from 100 per cent to more than 200 per cent if the crop bought by this method is exported. The lowest interest I recorded in this system was 50 per cent and the highest 300 per cent, but that commonly accepted by the *fellahin* is 100 per cent.

If a *fellah* fails to pay the crop he owes the moneylender, the price is changed to the current prices for that season. In the previous example, if the 10 *manns* are not paid immediately after the crop division, they will be counted as a debt of ID 18/000, i.e. 10 *manns* of the current price 'on farm', ID 1/800 per *mann*. As cultivation is always very late and the crop is often affected by blight, the *fellah* frequently fails to pay all his *akhaḍar* loan. Some of the *fellahin*, having a very small quantity of crops left to them, refrain from paying back their debt on such terms, and arrange to sell some or all their crop secretly. The moneylender, in fact, cannot take the case to the *ṣirkals*, or to the government, as such exorbitant interest is considered unlawful. In many cases the Administrative Officer compels

[1] The literal meaning of the word is 'green' indicating that the crop is purchased while still green grass.

the *akhaḍar* moneylender to take only 70 per cent interest on the money he actually lent. Nevertheless, the *fellah* dare not sue the moneylender, because once he does, he will find no one to lend him money in the future.

Agricultural land is mortgaged when the *ṣirkal* or the *fellah* is in urgent need of large sums of money. There are three types of mortgage in common use.[1]

In the first type, the *ṣirkal* as mortgager gives one-third or a quarter of his net share of the crop as interest to the mortgagee till the land is redeemed. The mortgagee pays the government tax in proportion to the interest he receives, i.e. a third or a quarter. Bharan plot for instance, held by Salih Ahl Zayir Sakhar, the *ṣirkal* of Ahl Anaisi, is mortgaged for ID 400/000 with Bait Sayid Jasim is-Sayid Khalaf for a quarter of the *ṣirkal's* net share of the crop as interest, the mortgagees paying a quarter of the land tax which the *ṣirkal* has to pay to the government.

In the second type, the *ṣirkal* gives all his share of the crop of one or two agricultural seasons as net interest to the mortgagee and thereafter a quarter or a third every year as instalments in repayment of the debt. The government tax is paid by the mortgagee in proportion to the amount he receives from the *ṣirkal's* share.

The third type of mortgage, which is fairly common, entitles the mortgagee to retain all the yield of the land, but he has to pay the total tax required. Needy cultivators mortgage their small holdings in this way to meet an urgent demand for money. They usually compensate for their losses by cultivating outside ech-Chibayish, where cultivation is more profitable. The land continues to be utilized by the mortgagee till the mortgager has repaid all the debt. A patch of one *habil*, which under good conditions yields about one *tghār* (1500 Kg.) of great millet worth about ID 30/000 is usually mortgaged for between ID 10/000 and ID 40/000 according to the conditions of flood, the location of the land and other considerations.

Ech-Chibayish never sell property until they have exhausted the possibility of obtaining credit. They prefer to take loans first and when 'loans draw other loans', as they put it when by the system of *galab*[2] and compound interest these loans become beyond their financial capacity to repay, they sell their cows, canoes and rifles, usually to pay only part of what has become a great debt. In some cases the creditor requires security such as rifles, cattle or canoes against his loan. The value of such articles should be higher than the loan taken, and the creditor has the right to use the rifle or the canoe and to consume the yield of the cattle. When a large sum of money is needed, shops and agricultural lands can be mortgaged. Shops are mortgaged for a fixed term during which the mortgagee can use or receive the rent from them, and if the money lent is not returned, the shops become his property.

---

[1] Other types can be effected according to private agreements.
[2] See fn. 1, p. 111.

In my survey of 120 families, 76 (63·3 per cent) were in debt: 18 (23·6 per cent) took loans with interest, and 58 (76·3 per cent) took loans on mats. These debts ranged from ID 1/000 to ID 300/000, as follows:

Number of families in debt	Amount of debts (ID)
18	1-5
17	6-10
10	11-15
5	16-20
9	21-30
6	31-50
8	51-100
3	More than 100
Total 76	

The highest debt recorded among the three lower economic classes was ID 300/000.

The reasons for obtaining loans among the 76 families mentioned above were as follows:

Number of families	Reasons for obtaining loans
55	To provide food and clothing
8	Brideprice for a son
4	To provide food and clothing and to pay brideprice
3	To provide food and clothing and to pay for medical treatment
2	Two members of each were taken for national service, thus depriving both families of productive members, so they fell into arrears in meeting subsistence expenses
1	The head of the family lost a considerable amount of money in working as an agent of migration to a date-packing station at Basra
1	Buying a sailing boat
1	Buying clothes for the feast
1	Sending one of its members for prolonged medical treatment to Basra

Although many of the expenses requiring loans are occasional, such as those involved in brideprice, paying a lineage share in compensation and mourning ceremonies, the great majority (over 70 per cent) of loans are taken to meet recurring subsistence expenses. The size of debts arising out of such loans, however, is generally under ID 20.

Anyone who lends with interest is stigmatized as having given up tribal values, so that moneylenders are necessarily outside the community of 'good fellows'. Nor can anyone normally hope to obtain a loan from a kinsman or fellow clansman, simply because the vast majority are living only just within their incomes or are themselves in debt. It is no coincidence, therefore, that many of the moneylenders are *sāda*, the 'holy men' whose status, being validated entirely by supposed descent from the Prophet, is not a function of the degree of their conformance with tribal values.

The moneylenders in ech-Chibayish are the keepers of the big shops whose turnover is large enough to leave capital for loans. Shopkeepers making a profit of ID 3/000 per month or so, who may themselves be obliged to borrow, do not practise moneylending. There are about 30 shopkeepers who lend; about ten of them are almost professional money-lenders, this part of their business being more lucrative and important than their shops. Beside these shopkeepers, there are all the mat traders who by profession must advance loans, and the cereal traders who lend on the *akhaḍhar* system.

The figures showing the degree of indebtedness in the 120 families specially investigated show that the extent of indebtedness is widespread (63·3 per cent). But they also show that the degree of indebtedness at any one time is not very considerable and we might even estimate that it is not greater than could be met by the sale of the property of the families concerned if they were obliged to pay off the debt. This is especially true if one includes among their assets (as they do themselves) the prospect of bride-price on the marriages of their daughters. If my sample of 120 mat-weaving families is representative in this respect, then 63·3 per cent of the mat weavers (57·6 per cent of the whole population of the village) are in debt to part of the three top economic classes who in all represent 6·4 per cent of the whole community. The significance of these figures is that there is a very great difference between the incomes of the top economic classes and the rest of the population.

Although most of Ahl ech-Chibayish are in debt, the economy as a whole is solvent. The gap between the earnings and expenditure of the majority is accounted for in the profits of the shopkeepers and mat traders, and partly also by the rates of interest charged for loans. The moneylenders themselves are never at a loss to find money for the advances they make. Their own profits are certain, and the imports of ech-Chibayish as a whole are amply paid for by the exports of mats and cereals. The problem of indebtedness is thus reduced to a problem of marketing.

12

Conclusion

SOCIAL AND ECONOMIC STRATIFICATION

BEFORE 1915 there was a close correlation between the social and economic stratification of ech-Chibayish. The top social classes enjoyed the greatest wealth while the lowest had none at all. The retreat into the swamps with its restriction on cultivation, the advent of effective foreign administration and the consequent contact with the outside world led to the substitution of a market economy for the old subsistence agriculture. Most far-reaching of all in its disruptive effect on the old social structure was the abolition of the Shaikhdom, which had been the corner-stone of the whole system.

The clan of Ahl Khayūn had formerly enjoyed complete economic and political domination through their relationship to the shaikh. If any Khayūni needed money, he could collect as much as he desired directly from the tribesmen. Many of them were agents, deputies and vice-shaikhs, acting for the shaikh in collecting his dues and in managing his vast estates, and thus had access to wealth and power.

The 'holy men', though economically dependent on the shaikh, enjoyed high prestige and a high standard of living comparable to that of the shaikh's own family. Their support was indispensable to the shaikh, as a word from them justifying any action of his would ensure complete support from the common people.

At the other extreme, there was a correlation between low economic status and low social standing, as in the case of the slaves and the Ṣubba (Mandaeans).

The Ṣubba were iron-workers and canoe-builders, but being despised and regarded as religiously unclean, they were unable to withstand exploitation by the shaikh and his clan. Nevertheless, they did enjoy some security and protection from the shaikh.

Among the social classes so far considered, Ahl Khayūn, the holy men, the slaves and the Ṣubba, status was determined by birth and there was little that the individual could do to improve or weaken his position. But in the middle class, comprising the commoners and their clan and lineage representatives, there was some scope for individual achievement in the economic sphere. Even in these cases, however, status within the group was only to a very small extent related to economic standing.

K

In spite of the radical social and political changes which occurred after 1915, the stratification of the five traditional classes remained unchanged, except for the emergence of the new political functions of the ṣirkals, mukhtārs and councillors. There was a head to each clan and lineage but they had no authority and were mere tools of the shaikh. Under the new regime, however, the newly created ṣirkals and the lineage headmen acquired considerable political authority which enabled them to exercise a new influence in the community.

The adjustment of economic to social standing, which was part of the traditional structure, was inevitably disrupted. New economic classes emerged as a result of the social change, all the privileges of Ahl Khayūn clan were abolished and there was no-one in the village to collect dues for the 'holy men', whilst the slaves and the remaining Ṣubba were left free to migrate or to acquire property.

The prestige of the different social classes has been derived from different factors. That of the 'holy men', together with their political influence, derives from their claimed descent from Muhammad, the Prophet, and that of Ahl Khayūn, from their previous, but now extinct, military and political leadership. In the case of the ṣirkals and mukhtars, prestige accrues to their political office, through which they control their clans and lineages.

As far as the ajawīd are concerned, any member of Beni Isad can be recognized as one of them and enjoy the consequent prestige through qualities which are totally divorced from economic standing. It is only necessary to have 'many brothers'—be a senior member of a large lineage, and be known as khayir, 'good fellow'. (The latter means a reputation as a generous and peace-loving man, scrupulous in religious observance.) A member of the ajawīd must not be known as an adulterer nor as a thief. He must have bakhat (conscience) which he does not sacrifice for personal gain in his dealings with others. He should also have knowledge of tribal law and traditions, so that his advice is sought in discussing compensation cases and listened to in any matters of communal interest and importance. With all this, he should also build and maintain a guest house.

Members of the ajawīd enjoy prestige and exercise influence in the community through many privileges, chief among which are, firstly, the fact that they are consulted by the ṣirkals on every important matter. In such cases the ṣirkals call them into a council called 'amra and hear their views on cases of compensation, or they are asked to interpret traditions or unravel complex questions of tribal law, or even to create new precedents. Clan members seek their advice on every important issue, such as tribal cases, compensation cases, relationships with other clans, land problems and disputes. They are given privileged places in the guest houses, and in any assembly people must stand up to show their respect for them. Often they are given special concessions in crop division, and some ṣirkals, such as the ṣirkal of Ahl ish-Shaikh clan, leave their shares entirely to some of them, and take only half from others.

Though prestige in ech-Chibayish is generally the public recognition of the fact that the individual exercises influence, there are individuals who attain prestige but lack influence in the community. A commoner gains great prestige from undertaking a pilgrimage to Mecca and becoming *ḥaji* or to the shrine of one of the Imams and becoming *zāyir*. Or he may gain prestige from being a senior member of a big influential lineage. But this does not necessarily allow him to exert influence in the community. Neither money nor any other item of property in itself confers prestige on the owner. Most of those who enjoy the highest prestige and exert the greatest influence are very poor. Conversely, most of the wealthy people and members of the top economic class are without prestige or social standing in the community. There are examples of people who failed to attain prestige in spite of accumulating property and of many who even lost prestige in the course of building up a fortune. Four of the eight families of 'holy men', the top class in the social scale, are poor. The members of the *ajawid* are mostly mat-weavers and cultivators and often in debt, but they are far more influential than many of the rich men. Of the latter only those who are 'holy men' or Ahl Khayūn enjoy high social standing, and they only because of their ancestry and in spite of their wealth. A penniless 'holy man', in fact, enjoys very much higher prestige than a rich one. The poor members of the class of the *ṣirkals*, *mukhtars* and councillors are always called *ajawid*, 'the good people', while the wealthy business men are called *ahl is-sūg*, literally 'the people of the market' implying 'those who departed from tribal traditions to acquire wealth'.

A typical example of a man who accumulated property but failed to attain high social prestige thereby is Abid Ahl Mishad. From his early youth he had been employed in various despised occupations, such as fishing and shopkeeping. So he was regarded as one of the young men who had departed from the normal tribal pattern. Suddenly, during the war of 1939-1945, he became a rich man and within two or three years his property had increased enormously. But his social prestige did not increase. Abid Ahl Mishad remained where he was: just one of the 'market people', one who had sacrificed tribal traditions for the sake of 'filthy lucre'. Many with whom I discussed this particular example pointed out that '*ish-sharaf* (honour) and *li'tibār* (prestige) are not matters of thousands of dinars'. When asked, 'Then cannot somebody like Abid Ahl Mishad be one of *ajawid*?' they answered, 'Where are his brothers? Where is his coffee set or his guest house?'

Many actually lost prestige in the process of accumulating property. Marid Ahl Tahir was the son of a *khayir* ('good fellow'). When his father died, he left no fortune. He followed his father's footsteps and, like him, gained after a few years the reputation of *khayir*. Later, however, he worked with Bait Sayyid Khalaf, the two rich families of grain- and mat-traders and moneylenders, and made money; but by associating himself with these people and by neglecting the tribal obligations and the responsibilites of his social position he lost his good reputation. People began to consider him as only one of *ahl is-sūg*.

Nevertheless, property can sometimes be utilized to gain social prestige. Obūda is-Salman was an outstanding example, in his earlier days, though in his later life he demonstrates how lust for gain can undermine the same prestige. Obūda is-Salman was a messenger at the government house. A corrupt administrative officer made him a 'bribe agent', and thus he earned a considerable amount of money. During the war of 1939-1945, the same Administrative Officer, for reasons of mutual gain, gave him the lucrative position of official sugar distributor. Thus Obūda suddenly became a wealthy man. During the period of acquiring wealth Obūda paid great attention to tribal obligations and relationships. He built a magnificent guest house and members of his clan, Ahl ish-Shaikh, gathered there frequently to drink his coffee. He helped needy members of his lineage and some clansmen, and thus he built up a reputation of being a 'good fellow'. But Obūda lost all his laboriously acquired prestige in a land dispute because of his persistent efforts to deprive the family of Ahl Khishshan of Ahl Haji Sari lineage of their rights to a patch of land which they had helped him to detach from Rzaij Ahl Sayid, the *ṣirkal* of Ahl Ghrīj clan. He claimed that he had spent a large sum of money in the land dispute and unless Ahl Khishshan family paid him half the cost he would not recognize their rights to the land. By his mercenary attitude, Obūda lost all claim to be counted as a 'good fellow'.

STATUS EVALUATION IN TERMS OF OCCUPATION

Despite the great economic changes and the impact of the market economy, for the vast majority of Ahl ech-Chibayish a rigid system of status-evaluation in terms of occupation still exists. They deprecate any divergence from the accustomed economic pattern of agriculture, mat-weaving and cattle-keeping. They look upon some occupations as undesirable, and on others as despicable and to be totally shunned.

The respected occupations are cultivation and mat-weaving, while cloth-weaving, vegetable cultivation, the selling of fish and dairy produce and fishing expeditions are despised. Shopkeeping and trade are equally to be avoided. During my stay at ech-Chibayish, I was particularly interested in this matter and made repeated attempts to discover the criteria applied. I discussed it with various people, *ṣirkals* and commoners, and the following is a summary of their opinions.

The cloth-weaver is despised more than any other workman. Next comes the vegetable cultivator, then the fisherman, and lastly the seller of fish and dairy produce. None of Beni Isad, except Ahl Ghrīj clan, would give his daughter in marriage to a cloth-weaver or to a fisherman, and none of the tribe, even including Ahl Ghrīj clan, would give their girls in marriage to a vegetable cultivator. If one of the tribe is refused a girl as a wife he will ask in offended tones, 'Have I cloth-weaving or fishing in my ancestry?'

There is no generally accepted explanation for these attitudes except in the case of the selling of fish and dairy products, which are despised simply because they are practised by the despised Ma'dan. The *ṣirkal* of Ahl ish-Shaikh clan, the best informed man on tribal matters, was unable to give reasons for the contempt for cloth-weavers and fishermen. As to the vegetable cultivators, he thought that they were despised because they wander through the village selling their vegetables, and selling in this way is 'shameful' behaviour. Haji Jasim Ahl Mhammad, of Ahl Ghrīj clan, a famous arbitrator and a well-known authority on tribal law and traditions, also thought that vegetable growers were despised because 'They wade the waterways and roam the village looking for customers', and cloth-weavers because 'They have no clear tribal descent, and they are liars. Moreover, they are unscrupulous; they stole the Imam li-Hsain's earrings and gave evidence against the Virgin Mary when she gave birth to Christ, and did many other bad deeds which history has recorded.' It is noteworthy, however, that all the cloth-weavers of ech-Chibayish are of one lineage, Ahl Hlal, of Ahl Ghrīj clan, and all the fishermen also came formerly from this clan, although there have been some exceptions in later years as a few men from other clans, particularly of Ahl Anaisi clan, have, under pressure of need, taken part in fishing expeditions. But there were no cases of men of other lineages taking up cloth-weaving. Other people of the Ahl Ghrīj clan do not despise the cloth-weavers or the fishermen, and intermarry with them. All the vegetable cultivators are outsiders to the village. So also are the Ma'dan women traders. All the tribe, including even Ahl Ghrīj clan, despise them. Thus all the despised occupations are practised either by outsiders, or by members of one clan, Ahl Ghrīj.

It seems reasonable therefore, to suppose that the roots of the scorn for cloth-weaving, vegetable cultivation, fishing and Ma'dan trade lie in tradition and in tribal exclusiveness. Beni Isad are bedouin, and it is their tradition to distinguish themselves by their occupations from the local marsh people whom they conquered when they arrived in the region. This is characteristic of all the bedouin. Those who conquered Iraq in the seventh century and settled there, abstained from following any of the traditional occupations of the original inhabitants of the country—Nabataeans and others who were mainly cultivators, fishermen and craftsmen. They maintained their cultural differences and their status as 'lords', partly by means of such occupational distinctions. At the beginning they continued their traditional desert economic pattern of camel-breeding until some of them gradually changed from desert nomads to settled cultivation, while others retained their ideal economic life in the deserts of Iraq. Regardless of the various localities in which the bedouin settled in Iraq and irrespective of their varying degrees of adoption into the conquered

community, never, until recent times did they practise any of the trades
or crafts of their subjects.

In addition, as bedouin life is based on camel-breeding and warfare,
they despised any occupation which is inconsistent with this way of life.
Whenever bedouin are compelled to settle and to cultivate, they cultivate
only cereals, never vegetables. Traditionally bedouin never regarded vegetables even as food. To them cloth-weaving is as dishonourable a way of
earning a living as any other sedentary occupation; it is slow and in-
glorious compared with the swift wandering life of the desert. The same
applies to fishing. Obviously everything connected with fish and water-life
is completely alien to the desert culture and its uncertain water supply.
What is strange to the bedouin way of life is despised.

Ahl Ghrīj clan (the only one whose members undertake cloth-weaving
and fishing expeditions) was not originally a clan of Beni Isad tribe, but a
very small and weak tribe which lived under Beni Isad's protection and was
eventually affiliated and assimilated into it. The origin of Ahl Ghrīj is
obscure but it is known that they were connected with il-Fartūs, a Ma'dan
tribe whose original home is in the Amara marshes, and that they lived
with other Ma'dan tribes for long periods. The Ma'dan of the Amara
marshes undertake fishing expeditions and among those who have settled
and practised agriculture as well as buffalo-breeding, there are one or two
cloth-weavers in every settlement. Whatever the origin of Ahl Ghrīj may
be, they are held to have no bedouin ancestry. This explains why they
differ from the rest of the tribe as far as the despised occupations are concerned. Not only do Ahl Ghrīj practise the occupations which Beni Isad
scorn, but they do not practise mat-weaving and only a small number of
them practise cultivation, the two main occupations among Beni Isad.
Before Beni Isad had given up warfare, before they had even taken
seriously to agriculture, and long before mat-weaving had become the
principal occupation of the tribe, Ahl Ghrīj had already committed themselves to a livelihood based on hiring their labour for wages.

Shopkeeping, as also any other form of buying and selling, is scorned
mainly because it is incompatible with the bedouin ideal. The bedouin
should gain his living by the sword. All his values are those of a warrior
society, in which the two dominant themes are courage and generosity.
By displaying courage in war and so obtaining plunder he gains his livelihood. Through generosity he disposes of what he owns. To be mean
implies a want of confidence in one's ability to gain more plunder. Mean-
ness, therefore, is a synonym for cowardice. Nothing could be more con-
temptible than thrift, bargaining, or the slightest appearance of attaching
value to one's material possessions. There is no room for the virtues of the
successful merchant. In bedouin eyes the trader is the epitome of all that
is weak, cowardly and mean. The trader needs peace, husbands his goods,
and is sly in bargaining.

Thus the mere inheritance of the traditions of desert warriors might explain the Beni Isad attitude to commerce. But they are also subject to another influence, that of Islam, which, in a different context, emphasizes the same dominant values. Material possessions and all enjoyment of this life are ephemeral and to be despised, in comparison with the imperishable rewards of the next life. Many verses in the *Qu'rān* teach these values. For example: *Surah* XXIV, verse 37: 'Men whom neither merchandise nor sale beguileth from remembrance of Allah and constancy in prayer and paying to the poor their due; who fear a day when hearts and eyeballs will be overturned.'[1] *Surah* LXII, verse 11: 'But when they spy some merchandise or pastime they break away to it and leave these standing. Say: That which Allah hath is better than pastime and than merchandise, and Allah is the best of providers.'[2]

I have already quoted several remarks of members of the ech-Chibayish community which strongly recall the attitudes to trade and moneylending of European communities in the Middle Ages. The discussions of medieval theologians about the activities of usurers and of rich traders are repeated every day, admittedly in a simple form, in this present-day community of Muslim Marsh Dwellers.

THE CONFLICT BETWEEN TRIBAL AND BUSINESS ETHICS

Professor Daryll Forde's observation that 'the impact of new techniques often leads to socially destructive individualism and conflicts of loyalties'[3] is applicable to the fundamental economic changes which have taken place at ech-Chibayish during the last 40 years. Like other marsh communities in southern Iraq, ech-Chibayish remained for a long time separated from the outside world. Before the First World War only a few Persians ran small shops to sell cloth, tobacco, and a few other commodities. When, during the war, contact with the outside world increased, some of Ahl ech-Chibayish ventured to open shops or to take up business such as obtaining contracts to supply mats or cereals to the occupation authorities. The pioneers had to act individually and there was a strong conflict between the desire for gain and conformity with tribal traditions. It is significant that the pioneers were all either outsiders, members of other tribes who had been living with Beni Isad for a time, or members of the tribe with the lowest social status, servants of the shaikh's household, fishermen, ex-employees of the Turkish Administration and so on. In the beginning they suffered much scorn and humiliation.

It is not easy at ech-Chibayish to take part in business and at the same time conform to native traditions, for the two are often basically opposed to each other. Popular estimates of prestige cling to the old criteria. The business men have by the very nature of their work to give up guest houses, which involve loss of money and time. They tend to think and act individually, and to put business matters above tribal ideals. Indeed, many of

[1] Translation by M. Pickthall, *The Meaning of the Glorious Koran*, London, 1948, p. 361.   [2] Ibid., p. 585.   [3] *The Native Economies of Nigeria*, p. 30.

the business men at ech-Chibayish have confirmed the tribesmen in their belief that business is incompatible with tribal loyalty. A few examples may illustrate this. A member of the most respected clan, Ahl Khayūn, was involved in a money dispute with a slave in the village market. When the slave was insulted he returned the insult and defended himself by trying to throw a stone at the Khayūni 'business man'. This incident aroused much disgust, and the business man was criticized for losing his dignity with a slave, in the market, and for the sake of gain.

Another business man, a member of an esteemed family of Beni Aschiri clan, though he was rich and had a shop and half the ownership of a motor launch, was notoriously avaricious. Among other things he used to bring in ice during the hot season and sell it at very high prices. He and his son were once involved in a quarrel with an employee of the municipality, as a result of which the Administrative Officer sentenced both sides to a few days' imprisonment. Public opinion in the village was entirely against him, as he had degraded himself by squabbling over ice-selling; and his lust for gain shocked even the market people themselves. In a certain guest house I heard the comment, 'He deserved imprisonment because, as he was not a needy person, he should not have degraded himself to this degree. What is the use of money to a man if he loses his dignity?' Most of the assembled people agreed that no-one should try to influence the Administrative Officer to release him, for he needed a lesson.

Again, a motor launch owner refused to comply with the request of his ṣirkal to take him by launch to Sūg ish-Shyūkh, because there was a difference of one of two dinars between the money asked by the owner and the money offered by the ṣirkal for the fare. This refusal demonstrates how little the market people now care for tribal values if they conflict with the exigencies of business. According to tribal traditions, any ṣirkal must be respected and his wishes complied with. In this case the ṣirkal was also a member of Ahl Khayūn. The tribesman, therefore, was traditionally under a moral obligation to offer him any services he might demand, free of charge.

Business men have also aroused the indignation of the villagers by what is considered their unreasonable exploitation. The prices of the commodities sold in the shops are high, and the interest on money lent is excessive. The system of galab in the mat trade is considered by most of the mat-weavers as a cruel exploitation, and the system of akhaḍar lending is another constant source of complaint. Both are considered contrary to the teaching of Islam. Any sort of usury is strictly forbidden by Islam,[1] and both moneylenders and borrowers know and admit it. Ahl ech-Chibayish regard the market people as 'unfair' and as people who 'do not fear Allah',

[1] In the Qur'ān, Surah III (The Family of Imran), v. 131; 'O ye who believe! Devour not usury, doubling and quadrupling (the sum lent). Observe your duty to Allah, that ye may be successful.' Pickthall, op. cit., p. 81. See also Surah II, v. 275 ff, and III, v. 39.

because they charge interest. As the *akhaḍar* lending system is run almost exclusively by the six members of Bait Sayyid Khalaf lineage, who are expected, as descendants of the Prophet, to be very scrupulous in their religious observances, people are more than ever convinced that money and commerce are 'the greatest evil which has befallen ech-Chibayish'—an evil which makes even the *sāda* act against their faith.

The impact of the market economy has greatly disturbed the former relation between economic and social standing. It also reflects the existence side by side in the same society of two opposed sets of values, the mercantile and the tribal.

But it should be remembered that though members of the market group pay more attention to business obligations, they do not totally neglect tribal obligations; for it is in their interest to comply with these as far as they can. They observe clan and lineage obligations when they do not directly conflict with their business. They pay compensations, share in the expenses of funeral ceremonies and give gifts at marriage. Their clans and lineages, however, derive no special benefit from their wealth. The richest man of the top economic class does no more for his lineage or clan than the poorest member, since clan and lineage responsibilities and obligations are exactly the same for rich and poor.

On the other hand, the people of the market do not yet show any tendency to act as a distinct group, nor do they show any inclination to intermarry; they follow the customary principles of tribal marriage. One exception may be the stronger tendency to break the rule of the intra-lineage marriage, as they are in general more capable of finding brideprices for their sons and thus do not hesitate to seek the higher extra-lineage brideprices for their daughters.

The market people have not yet adopted wholesale a set of new values incompatible with tribal life. They are tempted by the exigencies of business to abandon certain tribal values, while still desiring to maintain their prestige in the eyes of their fellow tribesmen. Sufficient time has not yet elapsed to separate them into a distinct group, but with the increase of trade, extension of business in the village, and with more tribesmen breaking the barriers of the traditional economic pattern, this class may well come to form, in the near future, a social unit different from the old tribal one, not only in economic pursuits, but in all its ideals and values.

L

Appendix A

CLANS AND LINEAGES OF ECH-CHIBAYISH AND THEIR POPULATION

Clans	Population	Lineages
1. Ahl ish-Shaikh	4,500	1. Ahl Sawwad
		2. Albu Zdew
		3. Ahl Dhumad
		4. Albu Ayish
		5. Albu Mkhaiwir
		6. Albu Hmail
		7. Albu Abaid Allah
		8. Albu Mkhaimur
		9. Ahl Awaiti
		10. Id-Dlaifiyin
		11. Il-Bukhatra
		12. Albu Zahrūn
		13. Ahl Khazzam
		14. Ahl Rahi
		15. Ahl Rofa
		16. Ahl Haji Sari
		17. Ahl Shyā
2. Ahl Ghrij	1,263	18. Ahl Haji Yagūb
		19. Ahl Hlal
		20. Ahl Hmūdi
		21. Ahl Ish-Sharia
3. il-Hadadiyin	1,200	22. Bait Rshaida
		23. Albu Aīdi
		24. Ahl Shaikh Ali
		25. Ahl Hajwal
		26. Ahl Haji
		27. Bait Shnayin
4. Ahl Khatir	773	28. Ahl Khatir
5. Beni Ashiri	625	29. Ahl Abdil-Mir
		30. Ahl Abaid
6. Ahl Anaisi	487	31. Ahl Anaisi
		32. Ahl Is-Saiba
		33. Ahl Attab
7. Ahl Wnais	450	34. Ahl Haji Abdulla
		35. Ahl Shahaf
		36. It-Tirshan
8. Ahl Limabir	315	37. Ahl Limabir
9. Ahl Wais	155	38. Ahl Wais
		39. Bait Mhammad Ahl Rashid
Total	9,768	

Appendix B

THE following is a detailed study of two lineages of Ahl ish-Shaikh clan.

AHL HAJI SARI LINEAGE

This lineage used to be called Ahl Hilū lineage, after Haji Sari's father. When Hilū died he left three sons: Sari, Ali and Chwayid. Sari was the eldest and the richest, and distinguished himself and established a good reputation. Then he undertook a pilgrimage to Mecca, which added very much to his prestige, and from that time people began to call the lineage Ahl Haji Sari after him.

Ahl Haji Sari lineage is now composed of five sub-lineages.

In addition there are seven families adopted into the lineage all of which are of different lineages of Ahl ish-Shaikh clan. In this lineage there were twelve non-lineage wives, who are not included in the table below, and five lineage women who had married outside the lineage, but are included in their natal families. Five men each had two wives, four of whom were non-lineage women.

All Ahl Haji Sari lineage live together in a number of adjacent islands. They cultivate patches of land held by Rzaij Ahl Saiyid, the *ṣirkal* of Ahl Ghrij clan, and a few other adjacent patches. Haji Sari, the founder, is three generations back to the oldest living lineage members.

Composition of Ahl Haji Sari Lineage

Sub-Group	Family	Men	Women	Boys	Girls	Children	Total
A	1	4	1	2		2	9
	2	1	1			3	5
	3	1	2		1	3	7
	4	5	4			5	14
	5	1	1	1		5	8
B	1	2	6	2	1	4	15
	2	1	1			3	5
	3	2	2	2		8	14
C	1	2	2	1		5	10
	2	1	1			4	6
	3	1				4	5
	4	1	1			5	7
D	1	2	4	1	1	2	10
	2	2	1			1	4
	3	1	1			4	6
	4	2	1			2	5
	5	1	1				2
E	1	2	1	1	1		5
Total	18	32	31	10	4	60	137

Sub-Group	Family	Men	Women	Boys	Girls	Children	Total
Adopted	1	2	3			1	6
foreigners	2	1	1	1		1	4
	3	3	2			2	7
	4	1	1	2	1	1	6
	5	1	3	1			5
	6	3	3	1	1		8
	7	1	1	1	1	2	6
Total	25	44	45	16	7	67	179

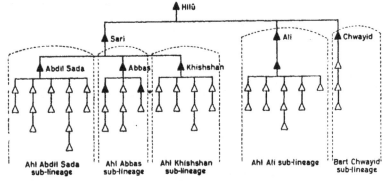

Ahl Haji Sari lineage

ALBU MKHAIWIR LINEAGE

All members of this lineage are descendants of Mkhaiwir, six generations back from the living elders of the lineage. In this case all members except the non-lineage wives are agnatic kinsmen. The lineage does not contain sub-lineage groups as every family traces its descent direct to Mkhaiwir.

16 non-lineage wives are not included in the table. Three women of the lineage who married out are included with their natal families. Four men were married to two wives each, and one to three.

Composition of Albu Mkhaiwir Lineage

Family	Men	Women	Boys	Girls	Infants	Total
1	2	2	2	1		7
2	2	4				6
3	6	2		1	5	14
4	1	2			2	5
5	1				3	4
6	3	6	1	1		11
7	2	4		1	4	11
8		6				6
9	2	5				7
10	5	4			4	13
11	3	4			1	8
12	1			1		2

Family	Men	Women	Boys	Girls	Infants	Total
13	1	1	1		2	5
14	2	1			2	5
15	1	1	1		3	6
16	2				2	4
17	5	5				10
18	3	1	2			6
19	1	1	1		2	5
20	1	1		1	5	8
21	2	3			3	8
22	2	4				6
23	5	4			3	12
24	1	1				2
25	1	1			2	4
26	1	1	1	1	4	8
Total	56	64	9	7	47	183

Bibliography

ALLEN, H. B., 1946. *Rural Education and Welfare in the Middle East*. London.

AMMAR, A. M., 1944. *The People of Sharqiya*. Cairo.

AZZAWI, ABBAS, 1936. *The Tribes of Iraq*, vol. 1 (in Arabic). Baghdad.

BALAYOF, D., 1948–1949. 'Fish in Iraq' (in Arabic). *The Iraqi Magazine of Agriculture*, vol. 3, No. 1, and vol. 4, No. 1. Baghdad.

BAYYATI, ALAA ID-DĪN, 1953. *Rights of Lease in the State Land* (in Arabic). Baghdad.

BELL, G., 1927. *The Letters of Gertrude Bell* (2 vols.). London.

BUXTON, P. A. and DOWSON, V. H. W., 1921. 'The Marsh Arabs of Lower Mesopotamia'. *Indian Antiquary*, vol. L.

CADOUX, H. W., 1906. 'Recent Changes in the Course of the Lower Euphrates'. *Geographical Journal*, September.

CAMPBELL, MAJOR C. G., 1949. *Tales from the Arab Tribes*. London.

CHESNEY, F. R., 1850. *The Expedition for the Survey of the Rivers Euphrates and Tigris in 1835-37*. London.

— 1868. *A Narrative of the Euphrates Expedition*. London.

CORRY, C. B., 1937. *The Blood Feud*. London.

DAFTAR, M. H. ID-, 1949. *Biography of Shaikh Salim Ali Khayūn*. Unpublished MS.

DARLING, M. L., 1932. *The Punjab Peasant in Prosperity and Debt* (3rd edn.). Oxford.

DEANE, P., 1948. *The Measurement of Colonial National Incomes*. Cambridge.

DIMMOCK, L., 1945. 'The Waterways of Iraq'. *Journal of the Royal Central Asian Society*.

DOWSON, SIR ERNEST, 1932. *An Enquiry into Land Tenure and Related Questions*. Letchworth Garden City.

DROWER, E. S., 1923. *By Tigris and Euphrates*. London.

— 1937. *The Mandaeans of Iraq and Iran*. Oxford.

— 1947. 'Marsh People of South Iraq'. *Journal of the Royal Central Asian Society*.

FHAMI, A., 1926. *A Report on Iraq* (in Arabic). Baghdad.

FIELD, H., 1935. *Arabs of Central Iraq*. Chicago.

— 1936. 'Marsh Arabs of Iraq'. *Asia*, August.

— 1949. 'Some Notes on the Albu Muhammad of Iraq'. *Journal of the Royal Central Asian Society*.

— 1949. 'The Anthropology of Iraq, Part 1, No. 2. The Lower Euphrates-Tigris Region'. Anthropological Series, *Field Museum of Natural History*, vol. 30. Chicago.

FIRAON, F. AAL, 1941. *Tribal Jurisprudence* (in Arabic). Baghdad.

FOOD AND AGRICULTURE ORGANIZATION OF THE UNITED NATIONS, 1949. *Essentials of Rural Welfare*. Washington.

FORDE, D. and SCOTT, R., 1950. *The Native Economies of Nigeria.* London.
FOSTER, H. A., 1936. *The Making of Iraq.* London.
FRANKFORT, H., 1951. *The Birth of Civilization in the Near East.* London.
FULANAIN, 1927. *Haji Rikkan, Marsh Arab.* London.
GECRE, H. V., 1916. *Lower Mesopotamia, United Empire.*
GHALIB, ALI, 1944. *Malaria and Malaria in Iraq.* Baghdad.
HAIDER, S., 1942. *Land Problems of Iraq.* London University Ph.D. thesis.
HALL, L. J., 1921. *The Inland Water Transport in Mesopotamia.* London.
HAMADA, S., 1938. *The Economic System in Iraq* (in Arabic). Beirut.
HARRISON, J. V., 1942. 'The Shatt-el-Arab'. *Journal of the Royal Central Asian Society.*
HASHIMI, T., 1930. *Detailed Geography of Iraq* (in Arabic). Baghdad.
HOWELL, E. B., 1922. 'River Control in Mesopotamia'. *Quarterly Review,* January.
— 1922. 'The Qanun al Aradhi'. *Journal of the Royal Central Asian Society,* Part I.
IONIDES, M. G., 1937. *The Regime of the Rivers Euphrates and Tigris.* London.

IRAQ
Administrative Report for the Muntafiq Division for 1919. Reports of Administration of Divisions and Districts. Baghdad, 1919.
An Introduction to the Past and Present of the Kingdom of Iraq. Baltimore, 1946.
Annual Report of the Directorate of Endemic Diseases, 1953 (in Arabic). Ministry of Public Health. Baghdad, 1953.
Census of Iraq, 1947. Directorate General of Census. Baghdad, 1954.
Climate and Weather of Iraq. Baghdad, 1919.
Law for the Administration of Municipalities, No. 84 of 1931. Statutes. 1931.
'Law for the Settlement of Disputes of State Lands Held by Tapu in il-Mintifiq Province, No. 40 of 1952'. *Iraq Government Gazette,* No. 3096 of 8 May 1952.
Report for 1918. Baghdad, 1918.
Report on the Administration of Justice. Baghdad, 1920.
Report on the Control of Rivers and Utilization of Water in Iraq (in Arabic). Irrigation Development Commission. Baghdad, 1949.
Report on the Political Situation in Iraq, 1918–1920. E. B. Howell, Office of the High Commissioner, Baghdad. 1920.
Review of the Civil Administration of the Occupied Territories of Al Iraq 1914–1918. Office of the Civil Commissioner. Baghdad, 1918.
Statistical Abstract, 1950. Ministry of Economics. Baghdad, 1952.
Statistics about Diseases for the year 1948 (in Arabic). Ministry of Public Health. Baghdad, 1949.
The Iraq Directory (in Arabic). Ministry of Interior. Baghdad, 1936.
Tribal Criminal and Civil Disputes Regulation. Government Press. Baghdad, 1926.
IRELAND, P. W., 1937. *Iraq—A Study in Political Development.* London.
ISMAIL, A. Q., 1934. *Twenty-five Days among the Marshdwellers* (in Arabic). Ali-Ahaly Newspaper. Baghdad.
ISSAWI, C., 1954. *Egypt at Mid-Century.* Oxford.

JAMALI, M. F., 1934. *The New Iraq : Its Problems of Bedouin Education*. New York.

JAMIL, M., 1935. *Comments on the Tribal Regulation and its Revisions* (in Arabic). Baghdad.

KEEN, B. A., 1946. *The Agricultural Development of the Middle East*. London.

KHAYYAT, J., 1948. *Principles of Agriculture* (in Arabic). Baghdad.

— 1950. *The Iraqi Village. A Study of its Aspects and Welfare* (in Arabic). Beirut.

LANDON, P., 1916. 'Central Mesopotamia'. *Journal of the Royal Central Asian Society*.

LEES, G. M. and FALCON, L. N., 1952. 'The Geographical History of the Mesopotamian Plains'. *The Geographical Journal*.

LE STRANGE, G., 1905. *The Lands of the Eastern Caliphate*. Cambridge.

LLOYD, S., 1943. *Iraq*. Oxford Pamphlets on Indian Affairs, No. 13. Bombay.

— 1943. *Twin Rivers*. Oxford.

— 1947. *Foundations in the Dust*. Oxford.

LONGRIGG, S. H., 1925. *Four Centuries of Modern Iraq*. Oxford.

— 1953. *Iraq, 1900 to 1950*. London.

MACDONALD, A. D., 1936. *Euphrates Exile*. London.

— 1936. 'The Political Developments in Iraq'. *Journal of the Royal Central Asian Society*.

O'DWYER, SIR M., 1922. 'The Qanun Al-Aradhi'. *Journal of the Royal Central Asian Society*, Part II.

PICKTHALL, M., 1948. *The Meaning of the Glorious Koran*. London.

ROYAL ANTHROPOLOGICAL INSTITUTE OF GREAT BRITAIN AND IRELAND, 1951. *Notes and Queries on Anthropology* (6th edn.). London.

SMEATON, W., 'Tattooing Among the Arabs of Iraq'. *American Anthropologist*, vol. 39.

SMITH, W. ROBERTSON, 1903. *Kinship and Marriage in Early Arabia*. London.

SOUSA, A., 1945. *Irrigation in Iraq, its History and Development*. Jerusalem.

— 1946. *The Development of Irrigation in Iraq* (in Arabic). Baghdad.

THESIGER, W., 1954. 'The Marshmen of Southern Iraq'. *The Geographical Journal*, vol. cxx.

THOMAS, B., 1931. *Alarms and Excursions in Arabia*. London.

— 1937. *The Arabs*. London.

UNITED KINGDOM:

Admiralty, Naval Intelligence Division Handbooks:

A Handbook of Mesopotamia, vol. 1. H.M. Stationery Office. London, 1918.

Colonial Office:

Review of the Civil Administration of Mesopotamia presented to both Houses of Parliament. H.M. Stationery Office. London, 1920.

Report on the Administration of Iraq, October 1920–March 1922. H.M. Stationery Office. London, 1922.

Report by His Britannic Majesty's Government to the Council of the League of Nations on the Administration of Iraq (9 vols.). H.M. Stationery Office. London, 1926.

Special Report by His Majesty's Government of the United Kingdom of Great Britain and Northern Ireland to the Council of the League of Nations on the Progress of Iraq during the Period of 1920–1931. H.M. Stationery Office. London, 1931.

Foreign Office Historical Section Handbooks:

Mesopotamia (No. 63). H.M. Stationery Office. London, 1920.

VAN-ESS, J., 1947. *Meet the Arab.* London.

WARRINER, D., 1948. *Land and Property in the Middle East.* London.

WILLCOCKS, SIR W., 1903. 'A Proposal for the Irrigation of Mesopotamia'. *Blackwood's Magazine*, December.

— 1905. *The Irrigation of Mesopotamia.* Cairo.

WILSON, SIR A. T., 1930. *Loyalties—Mesopotamia 1914–1917.* Oxford.

— 1931. *Mesopotamia 1917–1920. A Clash of Loyalties.* London.

WIMSHURST, C. R., 1924. 'Agricultural Problems in Alluvial Iraq'. *Journal of the Royal Central Asian Society.*

Index

Hyal Ahl Hsain, income of family of, 128-9

Ialiwi, 20

Ijilā, 20

Il-faṣil and *is-soda*: *See under* Compensation

Imans, devotion to, 12, 13

Incest prohibitions, 58-9

Incomes: *see under* Family; Fishing

in-Nahiya: *see under* Ech-Chibayish

in-Najaf, 12, 13, 64, 71n.; corpses taken to, 46

in-Nasriya, 3

in-Nazil: *see under* Ech-Chibayish

Iraq, 5, 7ff., *et passim.*; climate of, 5; map of, 6; marshland of, 5-7; Turkish administration, 27ff.

Irrigation, 18, 87

Ish-Shati, 19

Ish-Shwariya, 19

Islam, 12-13, 141: *see also* Shi'ah Marsh Dwellers

Jabir Ahl Mtashar, income of family of, 126-7, 130

khayir ('good fellow'), 34, 66, 74, 78, 79, 136, 137, 138

Khdhayir Ahl Flayih, income of family of, 127-8, 130

khishni, 101

khowwan ('brothers'), 51, 52.

Kubath I, Sassanian king, 17

Labour: communal work, 48, 51, 118; guest house and, 73-4; hired labour, 11, 20, 21, 140

Land: Beni Isad and, 83-4; clans and, 33, 47; land holding, 33, 116, 117-8, 120; land tenure, 83-4; *naqsha* system, 84; *ṣirkals* and, 84; *tāpū* titles, 83, 84: *see also* Cultivation

Law, 33; traditional tribal (*sowani*), 29

Le Strange, G., 17 and nn.1, 2

Levirate and sororate, 60-1

Li-Fhūd, 38

li-Hwaiza, Hor, 7, 12, 22, 29, 83

Lineages, 43, 46-51, 46 n.4, 145-8 *et passim*; agnatic, 44; guest houses and, 73-4; head of: *see* Mukhtārs; land and, 84; marriage and, 48ff, 58ff; membership and descent in, 46ff.; solidarity of, 4, 47ff.; sub-lineages, 47, 146: *see also* Adoption

Lishan, 95-6, 100

Lloyd, Seton, 8 and nn.2, 3

Longrigg, S. H., 18 and n., 30 n.2

Ma'dan, 8, 9, 10-11, 20, 21, 22, 44, 89, 91, 103, 139, 140; reeds and, 104, 107

Mandaean language, 69

Mandaeans. *See* Ṣubba

Marid Ahl Tahir, 137-8

Markets, 10, 110, 114, 116: *see also* Trade and Markets

Marriage, 4, 28, 48ff., 55-6, 57-8, 66; ceremonies, 50-1; contracts for, 57; gifts and, 50-1; *in-nahwa*, 50; intermarriage, 64, 69, 70, 139, 143; lineage and, 48-9, 58ff.; marriage by exchange (*ṣidiq*), 60; occupation and, 138-9; prohibited, 50, 61; sons and, 49-50: *see also* Brideprice; Elopement

Marsh Dwellers, classification of, 9-11: history of, 7-9; Ma'dan and non-Ma'dan inhabitants, 8: *see also* Euphrates; Tigris

Mat trading and uses of, 4, 63, 95, 108-12; export of, 109-10; four seasons for, 109; prices of, 107, 110, 111; three classes of persons and, 108-9

Matūg Ahl Shfaij, incest and, 59

Mat-weaving, 11, 84, 85, 86, 87, 91, 94, 95-6, 103, 104-12, 113, 119, 120, 123-4, 129, 138, 140; economic pattern of weavers, 120ff.; income from, 108; myth about, 107; prices and, 106, 107; techniques for, 106-8; uses of, 106

Meat, 93

Melons, 20

Midhat Pasha, Wali of Baghdad, 27, 30

Midina, il-, 20 and n., 64

Migration and labour, 21, 22, 91, 94ff., 98ff., 105, 107, 119; towns and, 13-14

Mijarra, il-, 29, 83, 86, 94, 106, 111

Milk, 92, 93

Millet, 85, 86, 87, 88, 89, 92, 106, 120

Mills, flour, 115

Mit'a, 57

Moneylending, 63, 85, 88, 101, 121, 131, 133-4, 141; loans, 131-4; usury, 63, 71, 141, 142: *see also* Debts

Mortgages, 131; three types of, 132: *see also* Moneylending

Motor launches, 19, 114

Mounds (*Īshān*), 12

Mudir in-nāḥiya (administrative officer), 30, 33 n.1, 34 38-9, 48

mujtahid, il-, 64

Mukhtārs (clan or lineage heads), 28 and n.2, 32, 33, 34, 35, 66, 72, 136; guest houses and, 73, 79

Murder, 52, 53, 58

mutaṣarrif, 30, 33 n.1, 34

muwamna, il-, 64

nāḥiyas, 33 and n.1, 38 and n.; tribes and, 38

Nasir Pasha Ahl Sadūn, 30

Obūda is-Salman, 138

Made in the USA
Middletown, DE
22 October 2022